Gallery Books
Editor: Peter Fallon

MOONSHINE

Jim Nolan

MOONSHINE

Gallery Books

Moonshine
is first published
simultaneously in paperback
and in a clothbound edition
on 4 September 1992.

The Gallery Press
Loughcrew
Oldcastle
County Meath
Ireland

ISBN 1 85235 096 2 (*paperback*)
     1 85235 097 0 (*clothbound*)

   The Gallery Press receives financial assistance from An Chomhairle Ealaíon / The Arts Council, Ireland.

Characters

McKEEVER
MICHAEL
REVEREND JOHN LANGTON
ELIZABETH, *his daughter*
BRIDGET
GRIFFIN

Time and place

Easter 1991. Ballintra, a seaside village in the south of Ireland.

The central location is a small Church of Ireland building of which Reverend Langton is rector. Other scenes take place on the beach and in McKeever's Embalming Studio and Funeral Parlour.

ACT ONE: Good Friday
ACT TWO: Easter Sunday

Moonshine was first staged by Red Kettle Theatre Company at Garter Lane Theatre, Waterford, on 29 October 1991, with the following cast:

McKEEVER	Tom Hickey
MICHAEL	Frank McCusker
LANGTON	John Hewitt
BRIDGET	Clare Dowling
GRIFFIN	Brendan Conroy
ELIZABETH	Jenni Ledwell
Direction	Ben Barnes
Design	Ben Hennessy
Lighting design	Roger Frith

The play subsequently opened at the Abbey Theatre, Dublin, on 26 March 1992, with Alan Barry playing the part of Langton.

Publisher's note

We have followed the text of Charles and Mary Cowden Clarke's edition of *A Midsummer Night's Dream*. The illustrations and decorations are by H. C. Selous.

for my mother and father

ACT ONE

Scene One

The church. Good Friday. Early afternoon.

Upstage centre, a simple wooden altar. Upstage right, a pulpit and, opposite this, an organ. In front of these a series of pews or chairs.

Doors lead off — one to garden and rectory, the other to vestry. When the lights come up, the church is empty and though it is early afternoon the space is dimly lit.

After a moment the doors swing open and we see MCKEEVER *with* MICHAEL *standing behind him. They are dressed in undertaker's black suits and* MCKEEVER *carries a bunch of flowers. He operates two distinct codes of body language — the one we see now, frenetic, jagged, nervy, and the other, the archetypal posture of the committed undertaker, still, erect, calm. Although he slips quite easily into the latter mode it is a performance, and we should see he is never quite at home in it.*

The entrance is a violent interruption of the fragile peace of the church. The doors swing open. A beat. And then MCKEEVER *enters with great gusto,* MICHAEL *trailing nervously in his wake.*

MCKEEVER Anybody home? (*Silence. Checks vestry*) Anybody home? (*Silence. Looks around and is about to leave but stops suddenly at door and returns to body of church*) Nobody home, Michael. (*Pause. Smile. Then heavenwards*) Oh I don't mean you, your Lordship. The Eternal Presence and all that. But not you. We know about you, don't we, Michael? (*Pause*) Or do we? (*Pause*) Is it the same as our lot? At home in his little . . . (*Turns sharply to altar*) No, he's not! Because there isn't one. (*Continues search*) Holy God! Nowhere to be found. (*Suddenly, to* MICHAEL) But always there when you want him, mind — that's the great mystery.

Anyway, business is business. No cock-ups this time. Work is work.

MICHAEL I'm frightened, Mr McKeever.

MCKEEVER And why wouldn't you be. In my experience, Michael, this first encounter constitutes the single most difficult aspect of our profession. On the one hand, the bereaved — bereft! On the other, the Funeral Director — directing. And *that* is what we offer, Michael — direction! The next of kin like headless chickens wallowing in a sea of grief. Meanwhile, you and me — *undertakers*, Michael — cool, calm, collected. Sympathetic, yes, but —

MICHAEL Aloof.

MCKEEVER Consoling, yes, and yet —

MICHAEL Detached.

MCKEEVER They don't pay us for our tears, Michael.

MICHAEL I want to go home.

MCKEEVER Well you can't go home. I didn't get to where I am today by going home, did I? We must confront our demons, Michael, confront them and —

MICHAEL Overcome them.

MCKEEVER Good! Anyway, you're not the only one who's nervous, we're all nervous. We're out of touch, that's all. Five months to the day since we buried Mrs Brady.

MICHAEL In the wrong graveyard.

MCKEEVER An accident, Michael. Could've happened to anyone.

MICHAEL They were very upset.

MCKEEVER (*Peeved*) I'm sure Mrs Brady didn't mind. Anyway, that's all in the past now, Michael — we must turn our minds to what is before us. He did say one o'clock, didn't he?

MICHAEL I think so.

MCKEEVER (*Glares at him*) You think so?

MICHAEL Is McKeever there? says he. He is, says I, but busy at the costumes for the play and on no account to be interrupted.

MCKEEVER I think we might have made an exception in this case, Michael.

MCKEEVER *On no account*, you said. Them costumes is important too, y'know.

MCKEEVER Of course, Michael, of course.

MICHAEL That was all. Ask him so, says he, to call and see me at wan o'clock. Tell him it's about Mrs Langton, says he.

MCKEEVER Indeed it is, Michael. All about Mrs Langton. And I'm sure Reverend Langton will be with us at any moment. Now, positions. You here like so, hands like this.

He stands before altar, hands together, head slightly tilted. MICHAEL *copies him.*

Authoritative, yet deferential. Wonderful! Just observe and imbibe, Michael — McKeever will handle everything.

MICHAEL (*Sternly*) Did you finish them?

MCKEEVER Finish what?

MICHAEL The costumes.

MCKEEVER Piece of cake, Michael.

MICHAEL But did you finish them?

MCKEEVER Course I did. (*Looks at* MICHAEL *who is unconvinced*) Almost.

MICHAEL We're meant to be on Sunday night, Mr McKeever.

MCKEEVER Yes, I know Michael. Eight o'clock, Parish Hall.

MICHAEL Half the playactors is gone missin'. And now Father Langton mightn't be able to do it either.

MCKEEVER Well observed, Michael. Just as well I know his lines, eh?

He climbs into pulpit and assumes the role of Theseus in A Midsummer Night's Dream.

Is there no play to ease the anguish of a torturing hour? Call Philostrate! (*Pause*) Come on, Michael.

MICHAEL (*Without conviction*) Here, mighty Theseus.

MCKEEVER Say, what abridgement have you for this evening? What mask? What music? How shall we beguile the lazy time, if not with some delight?

He descends pulpit.

See! Nothing to worry about, Michael — Mac will handle everything. (MICHAEL *glares at him*) Crede, Michael, semper crede! Faith! Faith!

He crosses to organ: sings and plays with great gusto, MICHAEL *drawn into it and joining in as* McKEEVER *soars to the climax.*

Faith of our fathers living still
In spite of dungeon, fire and sword
Oh how our hearts beat high with joy
When e'er we hear that glorious word!
Faith of our fathers, Holy Faith
We will be true to thee till death.

There's one in the eye for the Proddy Bluebells!

REVEREND LANGTON *has entered. In full flight,* McKEEVER *has failed to notice him.*

LANGTON Indeed.

McKEEVER (*Mortified. Pause. Weak smile*) Rector, I, eh, I didn't hear you coming in.

LANGTON Obviously not. Perhaps I should have knocked.

McKEEVER Not at all. Shur isn't it your own house — so to speak.

LANGTON So to speak. You know I haven't heard that one in twenty years.

McKEEVER I only ever knew the one verse.

LANGTON Proddy Bluebells, I mean. Do they still call us that?

McKEEVER Just my little joke, Rector. No offence meant.

LANGTON And none taken.

McKEEVER Well then . . .

LANGTON Hello, Michael.

MICHAEL I'm sorry for your trouble, Father.

McKEEVER Reverend, Michael, Reverend.

He crosses to LANGTON, *produces flowers from behind his back and offers them to* LANGTON.

I brought you these.

LANGTON (*Smiles*) Proddy Bluebells.

McKEEVER First crop. For the altar.

LANGTON Thank you. They're Margaret's favourite. (*Places flowers on altar*) I expect you know why I called you.

McKEEVER The 'phone seldom rings for a party. (*Pause*) The 'phone seldom rings. (*This is rehearsed*) I'm sorry for your trouble, Reverend. (LANGTON *turns to him. Then, lamely*) As they say.

LANGTON So am I. Deeply sorry. Only I'm not sure whether that sorrow is for her or me. Anyway, I thought it might be a good idea if we talked.

McKEEVER Yes. Yes, of course. (*Whips out notebook and pen*) Observe, Michael! (*By rote*) 'The efficient Director will make discreet, if meticulous notes, recording quietly and accurately the precise wishes of the bereaved vis-à-vis the disposal of the deceased.' Time of death, John?

LANGTON What?

McKEEVER I realise this isn't easy. But vital nonetheless. Time, you see, of the essence in these matters.

MICHAEL (*By rote*) Rigor Mortis, Odoration, Putrefaction.

McKEEVER Precisely. And so, John, time of death?

LANGTON How would I know?

McKEEVER Roughly.

LANGTON I'm not a soothsayer, McKeever! The doctors give her a few days at most.

McKEEVER The doctors. You mean . . . You mean Margaret isn't dead?

LANGTON Not yet. Sorry to disappoint you.

McKEEVER Yes. I mean no. Not at all. (*Turning to* MICHAEL) Only I thought . . .

MICHAEL He didn't say that. He didn't say she was dead.

McKEEVER (*Straining*) Oh. I see. Right. Well. Well, that's different, isn't it? That's very different.

LANGTON I had hoped we might anticipate the arrangements, McKeever. (*Disparaging*) I can see I was being optimistic.

McKEEVER No, no, no. Not at all. Very wise, John. The early bird, as they say, catches the worm. (LANGTON *glares at him*) Yes. Well then.

MICHAEL   Can I go now, Mr McKeever?

McKEEVER   Yes. Yes, I . . . I think that will be all for the moment, Michael.

MICHAEL   I'll see ye later so.

He goes to exit, stops.

The rehearsal's at eight o'clock, Father.

MICHAEL *exits.*

McKEEVER   Reverend, Michael, Reverend. I'm sorry, John. It seems I've cocked up again.

LANGTON   (*Smiles*) You've done worse, Mac. She's all but gone anyway. (*Crosses to organ*) It was good to hear it played again.

McKEEVER   If not exactly the right song.

LANGTON   Soon enough it will be the clatter of pinball machines and the squelch of sweaty bodies fighting it out over the volleyball net. I assure you, that's a far more daunting prospect than your somewhat discordant version of 'Faith of Our Fathers'.

McKEEVER   Discordant. Lovely word that. (*Pause*) Curtains so, is it, Rector?

LANGTON   (*Irritated*) John.

McKEEVER   The Baptist. Throwing in the ghost then, are we? Giving up the towel?

LANGTON   I'm tired of fighting, Mac. Anyway, it's no business of yours.

McKEEVER   That so? Didn't think your supporters were that thick on the ground.

LANGTON   I'm sorry. I didn't mean that.

McKEEVER   Doesn't matter. It's a shame to see it close, that's all.

LANGTON   Not of my making.

McKEEVER   Yes, I know. This church. Your lot. Not like ours. No . . . display. No . . . ostentation. I like that. If it wasn't for the business I'd think of converting. People around here mightn't think much of a Protestant undertaker.

LANGTON   The dead wouldn't mind.

MCKEEVER   They never do. It's the living that bother me.

LANGTON   Anyway, what makes you think we'd have you.

MCKEEVER   Your cup is not exactly overflowing, is it?

LANGTON   Miss Martyn finally cracked. She was the last, you know. Poor dear dotty Miss Martyn. Came cycling up to the rectory last week to announce she was going to Kiltown Church on Sunday with the rest of them. To be honest, I was somewhat relieved. They'd been going down like flies since Christmas until, in the end, there was just the two of us, our mutual embarrassment hovering in the air between us. It's no use, she said, they've beaten us. And do you know, Mac, I think they have.

MCKEEVER   And so . . . my brave Lord Langton — the gallant loser.

LANGTON   No. Just the loser. I stood at that altar last Sunday and waited. I waited, even though I knew no one would come. But nothing. Silence falling on silence.

MCKEEVER   Except for Big Daddy.

LANGTON   What?

MCKEEVER   Himself. The man above. Holy Goddo. He was here.

LANGTON   Was he?

MCKEEVER   Still is.

Silence. LANGTON *picks up flowers.*

LANGTON   You didn't know Margaret very well, did you?

MCKEEVER   No.

LANGTON   No one ever really did. In the end, I suspect, not even me. She was Ruth. Ruth amidst the alien corn. She hated this place with a vengeance. She never quite belonged, you see. None of us did, I suppose, but at least I had the comfort of the tribe. Margaret was an outcast, even among her own. The night my daughter left she decided she'd had enough. My wife is a remarkably determined woman, Mac, and with the invaluable assistance of Mr John Haig's whisky, it looks as though she's finally going to get her way. (*Silence*) I'm sorry. You shouldn't have to listen to this.

MCKEEVER   The necessary process of grief. I've observed the phenomenon and even endured it once or twice. Do please continue.

LANGTON There's nothing more to say. I'm tired, Mac. After Elizabeth left, this church and Margaret were my only certainties. Now it seems I'm going to lose both.

McKEEVER Death in my experience does have a certain air of finality about it. I'd hardly have thought the Commission on Church buildings was in the same league.

LANGTON What do you suggest I do? Hold a sit-in? Preach to an empty church?

McKEEVER 'Wherever two or three are gathered . . . '

LANGTON There aren't two or three. There's nobody left.

McKEEVER They'll come back.

LANGTON Will they?

McKEEVER Who leads the flock, Rector? The shepherd or the sheep?

LANGTON The sheep have gone, Mac. When we came here there were one hundred and ten parishioners. In five years that number was halved and on Christmas morning last, for what was supposed to be the final service in this church, there were just twenty souls left. (*Pause*) You can't argue with those statistics.

McKEEVER But you did. Langton's last stand. An act of faith, hope and love, all rolled into one.

LANGTON Or maybe nothing more than a foolish and futile gesture.

McKEEVER Not at all.

LANGTON I met the Commissioners and spoke at length and passionately about a condition for which there are no statistics — the mystery by which an emasculated and isolated community was, each week, and if only for an hour, united and strengthened by their presence under this roof. They heard my case. But we live in a cold climate. The church would close. (*Pause*) They made their decision, Mac. Not just the authorities, but the people. For the first time in my life I'd said no. I told them as long as any one of them would worship in this church, I would be there with them. Now there's nobody left. I'll do as I'm bid.

McKEEVER It's Good Friday, John. Christ died at three o'clock. I'm sure you'll wish to commemorate the event.

LANGTON   No one will come.

MCKEEVER   Someone will. (*Smiles*) Wait and see. And when Margaret dies, you'll bury her here, John. Because you have to.

LANGTON   No. That's what I wanted to tell you. The church in Kiltown will receive her remains.

MCKEEVER   We'll see.

LANGTON   (*Warning*) Mac . . .

MCKEEVER   I shall make the necessary arrangements. Leave everything in my capable hands.

> *He goes to exit, stops.*

By the way, John, Michael mentioned the rehearsal. I, eh . . . I don't suppose . . . (LANGTON's *look tells him everything he needs to know*) I understand, John. The real theatre is often elsewhere, isn't it? I'll talk to you later.

> MCKEEVER *exits.* LANGTON *watches him go. A beat before the lights begin to fade.*

ACT ONE

Scene Two

A beach. As lights come up on this area, sound of train slowly gathering speed, building, and then fading to sound of waves crashing on shoreline. MICHAEL, *alone, squatting in the sand, staring out to sea. Early afternoon. Good Friday.*

MICHAEL (*Mantra-like as he continues to stare out*) Ardglass, Kilmore, Farranstown, Ardbeg. All change. Newport, Killowen, Raheen and Lismore.

> BRIDGET *enters, unseen by* MICHAEL. *She watches as he continues chant.*

Ardglass, Kilmore, Farranstown, Ardbeg.

He stops sudden, aware of a presence.

BRIDGET Howya?
MICHAEL Y'had no right to frighten me.
BRIDGET I didn't frighten ye. Be hard to frighten you.
MICHAEL Creepin' up sudden behind me. Y'had no right.
BRIDGET Amn't I as entitled to walk the beach as you are to sit on it?
MICHAEL (*Sullen*) Ardglass, Kilmore, Farranstown, Ardbeg.
BRIDGET All change!
MICHAEL (*Annoyed*) Newport, Killowen, Raheen, Lismore.
BRIDGET I thought you'd be at the Stations.
MICHAEL Station's closed.
BRIDGET Of the Cross, I mean.
MICHAEL First of January, 1974, me and my father on the last train. The snow was in the fields, my father was

crying, and I was happy.

BRIDGET Stations of the Cross. The whole place is at it.

MICHAEL I might go yet.

BRIDGET Personally, I couldn't be bothered.

MICHAEL And I might not. I'll have to see.

BRIDGET What're y'up to anyway?

MICHAEL Mindin' my own business.

BRIDGET You picked the right spot for it. That wind'd freeze the balls off ya. (*He glares at her*) Any sign?

MICHAEL Sign of what?

BRIDGET Sea giants.

MICHAEL No such thing as sea giants.

BRIDGET There is so. You told me yourself. Livin' in castles under the sea, you said. And on certain days . . .

MICHAEL (*Forceful*) I changed me mind!

BRIDGET (*Backing off*) Fair enough.

MICHAEL Mr McKeever was only fibbin'.

BRIDGET Was it him told you about them?

MICHAEL He was only fibbin'. I comes here every day since and never saw them.

BRIDGET They might be shy of you.

MICHAEL (*Final*) There's no such thing, I said. (*Pause*) That man's an awful fibber.

BRIDGET My Ma says he has a fertile imagination. Same thing, I suppose. D'ye want one? (*Cigarette*)

MICHAEL They're bad for ye.

BRIDGET I know they're bad for ye. That's not what I asked ye.

He takes one. They light up.

Sister Maureen caught me foggin' behind the sheds last week — read me the riot act, so she did. You'd think I was a bloody schoolgirl.

MICHAEL Y'are.

BRIDGET (*Miffed*) Yeah. Well that's not the point. Sooner I'm outa that kip the better. Mac says I could go all the way — (*He looks at her blankly*) Oh not like that, though I wouldn't mind. As an actress I mean. My talent leaves him speechless, he says.

MICHAEL You're not that good.

BRIDGET Shur what would you know. (*Pause*) Are ye lookin' forward to it, Michael?

MICHAEL Lookin' forward to what?

BRIDGET The play, y'eejit. Sunday night.

MICHAEL I don't know.

BRIDGET Course y'are. I can't wait.

MICHAEL Y'might hafta.

BRIDGET How d'ye mean?

MICHAEL All the playactors is leavin'. Four more went this week.

BRIDGET I know all about that.

MICHAEL And now maybe Father Langton too.

BRIDGET Many are called, but few are chosen, Mac says. He rings me, you see.

MICHAEL He does not.

BRIDGET Does so. All hours of the day and night too. To keep me abreast of developments, he says.

MICHAEL Did he tell you that Madge Power is after quittin'? And her the Queen of the Amazons.

BRIDGET If she did, what loss is it? That one couldn't scutter straight, not to mind act. He's asked me to play Hippolyta.

MICHAEL L*y*ta. It's Hippol*y*ta.

BRIDGET Well, whatever her name is.

MICHAEL And what did you tell him?

BRIDGET What do you think I told him? Shur what is it only a few passin' remarks. I'd do that with a belt of me cap. (*Leaps up*) You be Theseus. Four days will quickly steep themselves in nights; Four nights will quickly dream away the time; And then the moon, like to a silver bow, New bent in heaven, shall behold the night Of our solemnities. It means Theseus and herself are shortly to be married and she's greatly looking forward to it.

MICHAEL I know what it means. You're supposed to be Lysander's lover as well.

BRIDGET That's Hermia. I am. And I might be gettin' Helena too — she's in love with Demetrius, y'see, who's also in love with Hermia — on account of Bríd Flynn's mother is mad at her over failin' the Pre-Leavin'.

MICHAEL   No one will know who y'are. He gave me a bundle of parts as well. We'll be the laughing stock of the town.

BRIDGET   Shur you've been that for years. (*Silence*) I'm sorry, Michael, I didn't mean that.

MICHAEL   (*Furious*) Ardglass, Kilmore, Farranstown, Ardbeg. All change. Newport, Killowen, Raheen and Lismore.

BRIDGET   (*Gently*) Does that train ever reach its destination?

MICHAEL   Every train does.

BRIDGET   And we will too.

MICHAEL   Except the ones that crash.

BRIDGET   Mac says it's an act of faith. The whole thing, he says, is an act of faith.

MICHAEL   I know what he says.

BRIDGET   Anyway, let them laugh. It's supposed to be a comedy, isn't it? I think we'll be feckin' great. (*Awkward silence*) D'you want a kiss, Michael?

MICHAEL   (*Pause*) No.

BRIDGET   I thought you liked them?

MICHAEL   I do. Not here. Someone might see us.

BRIDGET   They're all above at the Stations. There's no one here only the sea giants. They won't tell.

MICHAEL   All right so.

> He remains where he is, closes his eyes. She leans over and kisses him. Once. He waits, eyes closed. She smiles, then kisses him again. He responds and she encourages him. GRIFFIN enters and observes in silence. BRIDGET places MICHAEL's arms around her shoulders. The moment is tender and gentle. GRIFFIN lets it run, then begins to whistle, savagely violating the embrace. MICHAEL breaks away, stands and turns away from both of them.

BRIDGET   What do you want?

GRIFFIN   What you want, be the looks of things. Only you won't get it off Scaldyballs there — will she, Scaldy? (*Pause*) Nope. (*He is enjoying this*) And shur, maybe he hasn't got it to give.

BRIDGET   Leave him alone.

GRIFFIN   You're the one was at him, girlie. Givin' him ideas above his station.

MICHAEL We were only lettin' on.

GRIFFIN And on Good Friday too. That playactin' must be goin' to your head.

MICHAEL (*Storms past* GRIFFIN) We were only lettin' on, I said.

GRIFFIN (*Grabs* MICHAEL *violently as he passes*) Steady, bucko! Don't want our leadin' man back in the nuthouse again. Do we now? (*Releases hold*) McKeever's lookin' for ye. You're to go up straight away.

BRIDGET The rehearsal's not 'till tonight.

GRIFFIN I know that, *girlie* — but this is another class of performance — believe it or not, McKeever's got a job on.

MICHAEL *looks at* BRIDGET.

BRIDGET Go on, Michael, I'll see you later.

MICHAEL *glares at* GRIFFIN *before rushing out.*

BRIDGET Who's dead?

GRIFFIN Advance sales — the Reverend Langton's wife is about to croak it. Begod the Proddies must be hard up when they're askin' McKeever to put her down.

BRIDGET He's not that bad.

GRIFFIN Isn't he? Tell that to the Brennans over at Lacken, the night he took the wrong body from the mortuary in Fintown. They weren't expectin' Auntie Josie to look like a blushin' bride, but that oul' fella's beard was a bit of a shock to them.

BRIDGET It was an accident. Could've happened to anyone.

GRIFFIN Or the time oul' Flynn the cobbler started to leak an' the priest givin' out the rosary above in the new parlour. Drippin' like a broken tap from the coffin, he was.

BRIDGET That was before he took up the embalming.

GRIFFIN That was *why* he took it up. Not that it's much addition to him — the bugger hasn't had a job for months. Still, it's no skin off my nose — whoever boxes them, they still have to go six feet under.

BRIDGET It must be a great skill.

GRIFFIN   Oh, I knows me stuff all right.

BRIDGET   Not that — shur a dirty dog could dig a grave. Embalming, I mean. Only I'm going to be an actress, I might've turned me hand to it. I could've been Mac's assistant.

GRIFFIN   From what I can see you're giving him every assistance as it is.

BRIDGET   (*Haughty*) I don't understand.

GRIFFIN   Don't think I don't notice.

BRIDGET   Notice what?

GRIFFIN   At the rehearsals — always on hand — if you receive me meanin'.

BRIDGET   If you paid as much attention to Shakespeare as you do to other people's affairs, we'd all be better off.

GRIFFIN   Affairs is right. Here, give us a pull offa that (*cigarette*).

BRIDGET   (*Looks at him, stamps out cigarette, is about to leave*) Pull your own — it's all it's good for.

GRIFFIN   (*Grabs her, pushes her down, straddles her*) Do you think so, girlie? Do you think so, hah? Well you might be surprised. You're not playin' around with Mikey the Fool now, y'know. Poor simple Mikey that doesn't know what it's for and never will.

BRIDGET   Let me go, Griffin.

GRIFFIN   We can have a private rehearsal too, y'know. I have the same prop as the embalmer.

BRIDGET   Let me go, I said.

GRIFFIN   I think we'll do the love scene. Act Three, Scene Two, isn't it — Demetrius falls for Helena. O Helen, goddess, nymph, perfect, divine! To what, my love, shall I compare thine eyne?

> BRIDGET *spits at him.* GRIFFIN *freezes, enraged. There is a moment when it seems he might hit her. He breaks away.*

GRIFFIN   Bitch! Fuckin' bitch!

> GRIFFIN *exits.*

BRIDGET   (*As he goes*) Act One, Scene One. The course of true love never did run smooth.

BRIDGET *exits. Lights down.*

ACT ONE

Scene Three

As lights go down on beach, they build slowly on church. Early evening, Good Friday.

ELIZABETH *enters. She carries a small suitcase or travelling bag, pauses briefly at entrance to take in the space, goes to altar, observes the flowers McKeever had early given to Langton. She leaves down suitcase and exits to vestry.*

MICHAEL *enters, looks around him, notices suitcase and approaches it.* ELIZABETH *returns.* MICHAEL *backs off.*

ELIZABETH Hello Michael.

> MICHAEL, *frozen, watches her for a moment. A sudden bolt towards exit.*

No! Don't! It's only me, Michael.

> *He stops, turns.*

Elizabeth.
MICHAEL I was sent for Father Langton.
ELIZABETH You don't remember me, do you?
MICHAEL I'm looking for Father Langton.
ELIZABETH Me too. I'm Reverend Langton's daughter. Don't you remember me, Michael?
MICHAEL No.
ELIZABETH I remember you. Your dad used to deliver groceries to our house. Sometimes you'd be with him.
MICHAEL I don't remember. (*Pause. Slowly, the trace of a smile across his face*) VIP 123.
ELIZABETH What?

MICHAEL   The number of the van. The grocery van. VIP 123. Me father was delighted. Because I *am*, he'd say, a very important person.

ELIZABETH   Him or you?

MICHAEL   (*Pause. Glares at her*) I have me own job now.

ELIZABETH   Oh! Good for you.

MICHAEL   That's why I'm here. For the photograph.

ELIZABETH   (*Bemused*) The photograph?

MICHAEL   Of your mother. Of Mrs Langton. She's dying. I'm sorry for your trouble. I'm to get a picture of herself from Father Langton and bring it straight up to Mr McKeever.

ELIZABETH   McKeever.

MICHAEL   *Mister* McKeever. I'm his assistant. We have to get a photograph for the memory picture, 'see.

ELIZABETH   What's that?

MICHAEL   We makes 'em look the way they looked when they were happy.

ELIZABETH   That won't be easy. I should think it's a long time since my mother was happy.

MICHAEL   We does our best.

ELIZABETH   I'm sure you do — Mr McKeever was always a perfectionist. In desire if not always execution.

MICHAEL   I don't know what you mean.

ELIZABETH   Nothing much. How is he?

MICHAEL   He's well.

ELIZABETH   You don't sound too convinced, Michael.

MICHAEL   He's well I said. (*Pause. Then a torrent*) We're doing the play and all the playactors is leavin'. He's not that well at all.

ELIZABETH   I'm sorry to hear it. Perhaps I'll see him before I go.

MICHAEL   You'll see him at the funeral.

ELIZABETH   Yes. Yes of course.

LANGTON *enters from door leading to rectory. He sees* ELIZABETH. *Silence.*

ELIZABETH   Hello Dad.

Silence.

LANGTON Elizabeth.

ELIZABETH The one and only.

She goes to LANGTON *and embraces him.*

MICHAEL (*By rote*) I'm sorry for your trouble. I'm to get a picture of Mrs Langton for Mr McKeever's perusal. Not too recent he says, something from the middle years, maybe with the trace of a smile.

ELIZABETH (*Sees* LANGTON *perplexed*) He wants a photograph of Mum.

LANGTON (*To* MICHAEL) Tell him I'll see to it later, Michael.

MICHAEL He needs it now, I said.

LANGTON (*Terse*) I'll see to it later.

MICHAEL (*Disappointed*) Very well so. That's what I'll tell him.

He begins to exit.

ELIZABETH It was good to meet you again, Michael.

MICHAEL You came on the bus, didn't you?

ELIZABETH That's right.

MICHAEL I saw you. From the beach. The bus came up the Seafield road. Y'had to come on the bus 'cause the railway's closed.

ELIZABETH The railway's closed a long time.

MICHAEL First of January 1974. My father was crying and I was happy. (*As he exits*) Because I was going on a journey, y'see. Far, far away.

He is gone. They watch him go. Silence.

ELIZABETH How is she?

LANGTON The doctors give her a few days. I alerted McKeever to this fact. It seems he won't be found wanting when the time comes.

ELIZABETH You said in your letter she'd been ill for some time. If I'd known . . .

LANGTON I didn't want you back here out of some sense of duty, Elizabeth. I still don't.

ELIZABETH You have every right to be angry with me, Dad. But

31

I'm here because I want to be.

LANGTON I'm not angry. And as for rights, Elizabeth, I abdicated those five years ago when you left.

ELIZABETH I didn't mean to lose touch.

LANGTON That's something of a euphemism, isn't it? The annual Christmas card and a bunch of flowers on your mother's birthday.

ELIZABETH I'm sorry — I know it's unforgiveable.

LANGTON I didn't say that. It isn't my place to forgive anything, Elizabeth.

ELIZABETH I backed myself into a corner, Dad. Left for reasons I couldn't explain, then stayed away because that was easier than trying to. I'm sorry.

LANGTON Let that be the last time you use that word here. Your sorrow is mutual, I assure you — but you're here *now*. That's all that matters. And I'm very glad to see you, Elizabeth. We missed you very much.

ELIZABETH I missed you too.

LANGTON We didn't talk much — your mother and I — but I know she never stopped thinking of you.

ELIZABETH You don't need to say that.

LANGTON Maybe I do. Maybe too much was left unspoken.

Silence. ELIZABETH *goes to window.*

ELIZABETH She loved these windows. The way on certain evenings the sun would catch the glass. God's light, she called it. (*Turns to* LANGTON) I'd like to see her.

LANGTON Of course.

ELIZABETH On my own, if you don't mind.

LANGTON Whatever you wish. She's at the hospital in Fintown, you can take the car if you like.

Silence. ELIZABETH *is about to leave, then turns back to* LANGTON.

ELIZABETH When you embraced me just now I remembered the smell. We each have our own, you know. Neither pleasant nor repulsive but uniquely our own. And yours is the smell of my childhood. I can't get it anymore.

LANGTON It will come back.

ELIZABETH No. Not now.

LANGTON Your room is just as it was. Nothing touched. All your
bits and pieces just as they were.

ELIZABETH Nothing's just as it was — you know that. (*Pause*) I
also heard about the church.

LANGTON As you said, nothing's the way it was. It's silly to fight
that reality, isn't it? On all accounts.

ELIZABETH Probably. But that never stopped you before.

LANGTON McKeever said someone would come today. I'm glad
it was you.

Lights fade in church.

ACT ONE

Scene Four

The office in McKeever's funeral parlour. Good Friday night. McKEEVER
enters carrying a mobile 'phone.

McKEEVER Ah, Father O'Flynn. McKeever here, how are you?
(*Pause*) And why wouldn't you be, with the day that's
in it. (*Pause*) It's about the hire of the hall, Father. As
you are no doubt aware, my company Pyramus and
Thisby Productions intends to present Mr Shakespeare's *A Midsummer Night's Dream* in the Parish Hall
on Sunday night next. (*Pause*) That's right, Father, this
coming Sunday. You will recall, of course, that I also
booked the hall for Thursday, Friday and Saturday, so
that my fellow thespians and I might rehearse there
prior to the presentation of our humble offering.
(*Pause*) Yes, Father, rehearse — I believe it is sometimes still the practice. In any event, it seems there's
been a clerical error of some description. On my
arrival at the said hall, some thirty-seven minutes ago,
I was greeted by the cacophonous, if undoubtedly
enthusiastic, rendition of 'God Save Ireland said the
Heroes'.

Now, Father, avant-garde is one thing, but I do not
recall the inclusion of this little ditty in *my* presentation of the Bard's opus. And so, Father, in short —
what is going on? (*Pause*) A double booking? (*Pause*) A
double booking? When? (*Pause*) But, Father, I booked
the hall for these particular nights two months ago.
(*Pause*) But how could that happen? (*Pause*) Father, do
you realise how important this is — the posters are
already printed. (*Pause*) Father, I protest. I protest in

the strongest possible manner. (*Pause*) No, I don't know who they are. (*Pause*) The what? (*Pause*) The Easter Rising Pageant Commemoration Committee! Jesus! I can hardly wait.

He slams down 'phone. BRIDGET *enters, clearly distraught.* McKEEVER's *mood and tone change radically on her arrival — a sort of feigned nonchalance.*

Bridget! Dear little Peas-Blossom Bridget — you got my epistle.

BRIDGET No, but your note was on the door.

McKEEVER (*Infinite patience*) Yes. Pull up a pew, Bridget. Let me take your jacket.

He goes around desk and helps her off with her jacket, allowing himself a fleeting glance of her breasts as he does so.

BRIDGET Thanks, Mr McKeever.

McKEEVER (*Absently throwing jacket into coffin*) Mac. You must call me Mac — (*Aside*) as in Flasher.

BRIDGET What's going on, Mac? There was another crowd rehearsing in the hall.

McKEEVER It seems the Easter Rising wasn't entirely successful the first time — they're going to do it again. With music.

BRIDGET How d'y'mean?

McKEEVER Never mind, Bridget. Let us not concern ourselves with mediocrities. We shall find another arena for our humble offering.

BRIDGET But we're meant to be on Sunday night — there's nowhere else.

McKEEVER The Lord will provide, Bridget. Now, what news of Lysander and Demetrius.

BRIDGET No sign o' them yet, Mr McKeever (*He gestures a reminder*) — Mac, I mean. I left the note on the door below in the hall.

McKEEVER Very wise, Bridget. No doubt they shall join us presently. We shall rehearse here tonight.

35

BRIDGET   In the funeral parlour?

McKEEVER   Why not? What is our quest, Bridget, in the presentation of this play?

BRIDGET   (*By rote*) The charting of those dangerous and mercurial waters between the islands of Truth and Illusion!

McKEEVER   Excellent! And here too, Bridget, a similar ritual is played out. When we present the deceased to the sorrowing multitudes, we are balancing the truth of our mortality with the illusion of restful sleep.

BRIDGET   You're a feckin' genius so y'are.

McKEEVER   I couldn't agree more.

BRIDGET   It must be an awful cross to carry — in a place like this, I mean.

McKEEVER   Though I wear the mantle lightly, I am ever conscious of its presence. (*Takes dress from drawer*) Helena's costume, Bridget — wear it with pride.

BRIDGET   (*Delighted*) Is Bríd Flynn gone then?

McKEEVER   Yes. Yes, I'm afraid so. It seems her mother is worried about her points. A minor setback. We shall triumph over all adversity — our faith will make us whole.

BRIDGET   Jesus! Hermia and Helena. (*Looks at him*) Oh, but I won't let you down, Mac.

McKEEVER   I'm sure you won't.

BRIDGET   The costume's lovely.

McKEEVER   Yes, isn't it? I ran it up last night on Mrs McKeever's *Brother* — her sewing machine, I mean. It was all she left behind, but one is grateful for small mercies.

BRIDGET   She's gone a long time now, isn't she?

McKEEVER   She ran away with a ballroom dancer — between the rumba and the turkey trot, I believe.

BRIDGET   (*Begins to undress*) You must be lonely after her.

McKEEVER   (*Mesmerized. Desperate to maintain composure*) Oh no. Yes. I mean, not at all. Of course. (*Turns away*) Oh Jesus!

BRIDGET   Is anything the matter, Mac?

McKEEVER   (*Facing away from her*) Matter? No, nothing's the matter! What could possibly be the matter?

BRIDGET   Good.

McKEEVER   Yes. Yes, very good.

The 'phone rings. McKEEVER *turns instinctively to pick*

it up, but quickly turns away when he sees BRIDGET.
She picks up 'phone and gives it to him.

McKeever's Funeral Emporium. How can we help
you? Ah, Sister June, thank you for ringing me back so
promptly. I should like to enquire as to the condition
of a Mrs Margaret Langton, whom I understand is a
patient of yours. What? Peggy, is it? (*Contemptuous*)
How intimate! (*Pause*) No, I am not a relative — her
mortician actually. I rang to enquire if Mrs Langton
was still with us. (*Pause*) Good. Well, no harm in
checking. Time — a vital factor in these matters. You'd
be surprised, I'm telling you, how quickly old Rigor
Mortis gets his grip on you. (*Pause*) Tell me, Sister,
has 'Peggy' had any visitors this evening? (*Pause*)
Elizabeth. Yes. (*Pause*) No reason really. (*Pause*) No.
No. I assure you everything's under control at this
end. (*Looks at* BRIDGET *undressing*) Just waiting for the
off, as they say. (*Pause*) The wrong graveyard? Yes,
that was rather unfortunate, wasn't it? Still, as the
Good Lord said to his disciples over dinner one night:
Show me the man, says he, show me the man who
hasn't made a mistake — (*She hangs up*) And a happy
Good Friday to you too, Sister! (*Turns to face* BRIDGET)

BRIDGET What do you think?
McKEEVER (*Enchanted*) Very — becoming. (*Checks himself*) I think
we should rehearse, that's what I think.
BRIDGET But there's no one here yet.
McKEEVER Never mind that — no time to lose. Act Two, Scene
Two — Helena's first scene with Demetrius. (*Scripts
out*) She follows him into the wood. I'll play Demet-
rius and you — (*He looks at her. Lost*)
BRIDGET Yes, Mac?
McKEEVER You. Yes. (*Snaps out of it*) You play Helena. (*Gives her
a script. Searches for page numbers*)
BRIDGET Page forty-eight, Mr McKeever. I had a feeling that
Flynn wan wouldn't last the course.
McKEEVER Many are called, Bridget — but few are chosen. So.
Here we are. The enchanted forest. Demetrius rushes
in . . .

BRIDGET Pursued by the lovelorn Helena.

> MCKEEVER *stands back and makes a bold furious entrance. They act out the following scene, Act Two, Scene Two, from* A Midsummer Night's Dream. *We see how the events of the 'scene' are parallelled with the cat and mouse game between* MCKEEVER *and* BRIDGET, BRIDGET *using Helena's lines to make clear her own intentions towards* MCKEEVER. MCKEEVER *resists her advances, though every bone in his body would wish it otherwise. Throughout the sequence, she physically pursues* MCKEEVER, *who desperately tries to avoid her clutches.*

MCKEEVER (*As Demetrius*) I love thee not, therefore pursue me not.
Where is Lysander and fair Hermia?
The one I'll slay, the other slayeth me.
Thou told'st me they were stol'n into this wood;
And here am I, and wood within this wood,
Because I cannot meet my Hermia.
Hence! Get thee gone, and follow me no more.

BRIDGET (*As Helena*) You draw me, you hard-hearted adamant;
But yet you draw not iron, for my heart
Is true as steel: leave you your power to draw,
And I shall have no power to follow you.

MCKEEVER Do I entice you? Do I speak you fair?
Or, rather, do I not in plainest truth
Tell you, I do not nor I cannot love you?

BRIDGET And even for that do I love you the more. (*Leaps onto desk*)

MCKEEVER (*Alarmed*) Now take it easy, Bridget.

BRIDGET I am your spaniel; and, Demetrius,
The more you beat me, I will fawn on you:
Use me but as your spaniel, spurn me, strike me,
Neglect me, lose me; only give me leave,
Unworthy as I am, to follow you.
What worser place can I beg in your love
(And yet a place of high respect with me)
Than to be used as you use your dog?

She throws away script. Grabs McKEEVER *and violently lowers him onto desk.*

McKEEVER Bridget! Tempt not too much the hatred of my spirit;
For I am sick when I do look on thee.
BRIDGET And I am sick when I look not on you.

She straddles him and begins to unbutton his shirt.

McKEEVER You do impeach your modesty too much,
To leave the city, and commit yourself
Into the hands of one that loves you not;
To trust the opportunity of night,
And the ill-counsel of a desert place,
With the rich worth of your virginity.
BRIDGET Your virtue is my privilege for that.
It is not night when I do see your face,
Therefore I think I am not in the night
Nor doth this wood lack worlds of company,
For you in my respect are all the world:
Then how can it be said I am alone,
When all the world is here to look on me?

> GRIFFIN *and* MICHAEL *have entered. They arrive on the line 'Nor doth this wood lack worlds of company'. They watch,* GRIFFIN *with some amusement,* MICHAEL *awe-struck, from the lines 'Then how can it be said I am all alone, When all the world is here to look on me' after which* BRIDGET, *consumed, as they say, with passion, plants a smacker on* McKEEVER's *lips.*

McKEEVER (*Drops script. Surrenders*) I'll run from thee and hide me in the brakes,
And leave thee to the mercy of wild beasts.
MICHAEL We were thrown out of the hall.

> McKEEVER *and* BRIDGET *freeze, then struggle quickly to regain, so to speak, their composure.* GRIFFIN *sneers in amusement,* MICHAEL *caught somewhere between jealousy and awe.*

GRIFFIN   Sorry we're late, boss — though I can see we didn't keep ye waitin'.

McKEEVER   No. Time is of the essence, Griffin. We were just running over Bridget's lines, weren't we, Bridget?

BRIDGET   I knew them all, Michael.

McKEEVER   Yes. You certainly did. Hello Michael — all set then, are we?

MICHAEL   We were thrown out of the hall.

McKEEVER   By the soldiers of destiny, no doubt.

GRIFFIN   Fine lookin' pageant. Uniforms and everything.

MICHAEL   They're on Sunday night.

McKEEVER   So I hear.

GRIFFIN   Wanted me to take a part.

BRIDGET   Yeah. You'd make a great tricolour.

MICHAEL   *They're on Sunday night,* I said. They've taken over the hall.

GRIFFIN   But I said no. (*For* BRIDGET's *benefit*) I'm on the payroll elsewhere, says I. Professional like. Not like some.

MICHAEL   What I want to know, Mr McKeever . . .

McKEEVER   Now take it easy, Michael.

MICHAEL   . . . is where does that leave us.

GRIFFIN   Down the tubes, Mikey; if y'ask me.

BRIDGET   Shut up, Griffin. No one's askin' you anythin'.

McKEEVER   Trust me, Michael. Have I ever let you down? (MICHAEL *unconvinced. Quickly*) Don't answer that. These little setbacks. Part and parcel of the creative process. A challenge. Not an obstacle. Trust me. Now, who are we missing?

GRIFFIN   The Flynn youngwan. Is she coming?

McKEEVER   Of course she is.

BRIDGET   (*Gesturing to dress*) Mac . . .

McKEEVER   No. No, the Flynn youngwan won't be with us, I'm afraid.

GRIFFIN   Joe Brennan's pulled out as well. He said to tell you.

McKEEVER   Very kind of him to let me know. Brennan's no loss anyway. Michael, you play Egeus.

MICHAEL   But I'm already playing Philostrate, Puck, Bottom, Pyramus and a fairy in Titania's service.

McKEEVER   True. Griffin?

GRIFFIN   Don't look at me, boss.

MCKEEVER I *am* looking at you, Griffin.

> MCKEEVER *closes in on* GRIFFIN. GRIFFIN *holds his ground.*

GRIFFIN Of course, I could be persuaded . . .

MCKEEVER I'll play Egeus myself.

BRIDGET But you can't play Hermia's father and her fiancé.

MCKEEVER Poetic licence, Bridget, poetic licence.

MICHAEL (*Quietly*) Madge Power is after quittin' too.

MCKEEVER (*Patience wearing thin*) That was last week, Michael. Last week's dross has already been turned to gold. And while we're on the subject of who's coming and not coming, you may be aware that Reverend Langton's wife is . . . indisposed.

GRIFFIN Indisposed? She's fuckin' dyin'!

MCKEEVER (*A withering glance*) Thank you, Griffin. For this reason I have reluctantly decided to replace him. I, myself, shall play Theseus, the King. A part for which I'm sure you'll agree my life's work has been a preparation. Now, can we begin?

BRIDGET But this is all there is, Mac.

MCKEEVER Yes . . . and more than enough.

MICHAEL There's twenty-two in the play, Mr McKeever. We'll never do it with just the four of us.

MCKEEVER Michael, I myself have witnessed *Romeo and Juliet* rendered with a dramatic personae of just two. Now *A Midsummer Night's Dream*. Purpose of quest?

ALL (*No enthusiasm*) To plumb the depths of those dangerous and mercurial waters . . .

MCKEEVER (*Exclaims*) Da capo! Con brio! Purpose of quest?

ALL To plumb the depths of those dangerous and mercurial waters between the islands of Truth and Illusion.

MCKEEVER Excellent.

GRIFFIN We'll plumb the fuckin' depths all right.

MCKEEVER Shut up, Griffin! Illusion and Truth, Michael. *Illusion and Truth.* We create the illusion in order to render the truth. And we *will* create it. Four or twenty-four — believe and you shall not be found wanting. Now. Act Two, Scene Three. Puck anoints the eyes of Lysander.

Clear the space and stand by.

> BRIDGET *and* MICHAEL *clear the desk and swivel chair.*
> MCKEEVER *sets out two chairs for rehearsal.*

GRIFFIN   Would ye have that few bob, boss?

MCKEEVER   That's what it comes down to, isn't it, Griffin?

GRIFFIN   Oh now. You know yourself. One professional to another, like.

MCKEEVER   Indeed. Here's your money, Griffin.

GRIFFIN   Somethin' else, boss. The rector's wife. Will she be wantin' a grave dug?

MCKEEVER   That is the normal method of disposal, yes.

GRIFFIN   Only with the church being closed and all . . .

MCKEEVER   The church is not closed, Griffin.

GRIFFIN   That's not what I heard.

MCKEEVER   *The church is not closed!* What you heard or didn't hear is thankfully of no consequence, Griffin. In any event, and as you well know, Reverend Langton employs his own gravedigger.

GRIFFIN   Not anymore he doesn't. Only I checked, d'y'see. Gorman went with the rest of them. I only mention it on account of I wouldn't like to see ye stuck.

MCKEEVER   I shall bear that in mind, Griffin. Now, we have a lot of work to do — Act Two, Scene Three. Puck anoints the eyes of Lysander. Griffin, you know your position, you're on the hillock. Bridget, you're at his feet. And Michael. (MICHAEL *mesmerized by* BRIDGET's *costume*) Michael? *Michael!* (*The spell is broken*) Puck approaches with the magic potion.

GRIFFIN   One more thing, boss.

MCKEEVER   Yes, Griffin.

GRIFFIN   What I was sayin' there about the pageant crowd wantin' me to take a part. I wasn't jokin', y'know.

MCKEEVER   Oh, I'm sure you weren't.

GRIFFIN   Last Sunday, there, after Mass. Himself corners me in the chapel yard.

MCKEEVER   Himself?

GRIFFIN   Father O'Flynn — the producer.

MCKEEVER   The producer?

GRIFFIN Yeah.

McKEEVER Ah. The penny drops.

GRIFFIN You're the spittin' image of Joseph Mary Plunkett, says he. (*Pause*) You know, Plunkett, one of the dead heroes.

McKEEVER I can think of nothing more suited to your talents. You must have been sorely tempted.

GRIFFIN I was, boss, and no denyin' it. But I stuck by ye, didn't I? I kept the faith.

McKEEVER Indeed you did, Griffin. (*Withering*) And I'm so very, very grateful! (*A pause.* GRIFFIN *uncertain how to take this*) Now, stand by — for magic!

As he says this, he clicks his fingers and we lose the lights on this scene.

ACT ONE

Scene Five

The church. Midnight. As lights snap to blackout on funeral parlour
we bring them slowly up on church as ELIZABETH *enters from vestry*
with candle. She places candle on altar and sits in chair or pew. After
a moment or two McKEEVER *enters. He watches* ELIZABETH *briefly*
before speaking.

McKEEVER   The prodigal daughter . . . has returned.

ELIZABETH   Hello Mac.

McKEEVER   Yes. Oh yes. And her name . . . shall be called
Elizabeth.

ELIZABETH   Long time no see. I . . . I just got back today. Would
have called round but I had to go to the hospital. I
gather you know about Mum.

McKEEVER   Yes.

ELIZABETH   Dad wrote to me. I got here as soon as I could.

McKEEVER   Yes. No news like bad news — as the fella said. Used
to be the way with telegrams once. Oh yes, I'm telling
you — run like the clappers from the postboy's bike,
no good news ever came in a telegram. Not strictly
true, of course, but in general. (*Pause*) And the father.
The father. Always on the lookout for them, one step
ahead of the posse, waiting for the corpse to come
home. Over to Shannon for the American ones, the
English came up on the *Princess Maud*. Sometimes I
used to go with him for the spin and he'd be singing
the whole way home. Singing, if you don't mind.
Because he was happy, you see. Only you're not
supposed to be! You can't be singing 'The Whistling
Gypsy' at the head of a funeral, beltin' out an aria on
Shop Street, with someone's Auntie Mary in the back

44

of the hearse. No siree, not the ticket. So! Only on the open road where no one could tell him otherwise. (*Pause*) Yes. Where did that come from?

ELIZABETH (*Laughing*) You were talking about telegrams.

McKEEVER Telegrams. Yes. Mind if I join you?

ELIZABETH Of course not.

McKEEVER (*Taking a pew opposite her*) Only I was passing, you see. My perambulations. And the lights through the colouredy windows catching my eye. Will those who pass this way today a little prayer to Jesus say.

ELIZABETH It's good to see you, Mac.

McKEEVER Yes? You too. Good Friday. He's over the worst now.

ELIZABETH Who?

McKEEVER Jesus. All downhill from here. Sunday's the big day of course. Res-urrection. Lovely word that.

ELIZABETH You haven't changed much.

McKEEVER You have. I can tell. Older.

ELIZABETH Five years older.

> *Pause. She gets up, moves away. Change-the-subject time.*

So. How have you been?

McKEEVER Never better. (*Sharply*) And you?

ELIZABETH I met Michael earlier. He tells me you're still putting on the plays.

McKEEVER Still *trying* to. Nearly there this time though. Sunday night. Parish Hall. No, scrub that. Not now. (*Looking around*) Somewhere.

ELIZABETH What are you doing?

McKEEVER *A Midsummer Night's Dream.* Thought it might be appropriate.

ELIZABETH At Easter?

McKEEVER Precisely.

ELIZABETH God, you really haven't changed, have you? (*Lightly*) No wonder the drama society got rid of you.

McKEEVER Philistines. And they didn't get rid of me. I *resigned*.

ELIZABETH For assaulting Mr Gibson, I believe.

McKEEVER Long overdue. Last time he tells me I'm taking things too seriously.

45

ELIZABETH   You broke his jaw, Mac — he might have a point.

McKEEVER   Probation Act applied. Fifty quid in the poor box. No more to be said. (*Pause*) So what's the answer?

ELIZABETH   What?

McKEEVER   To *my* question. So, how have you been, says you. Never better, says I. And *you*?

ELIZABETH   (*Laughs*) Persistent as ever. I'm all right, Mac.

McKEEVER   What have you been up to? As they say.

ELIZABETH   Not a lot. Got a job. Went to college. Got another job. Anyway, I explained all that in my letters — to which, of course, you never replied.

McKEEVER   No. Daddy must have been surprised to see you.

ELIZABETH   He was, a little.

McKEEVER   And Peggy? That's what they call her above in the hospital. (*Sarcastic*) Very touching.

ELIZABETH   She didn't recognise me. It would have been nice to say hello.

McKEEVER   And goodbye.

ELIZABETH   It's as though she were already dead. I'm sure you're familiar with the condition.

McKEEVER   The death trance. A sort of rehearsal for the real thing.

ELIZABETH   There were things I wanted to tell her. Nothing grandiose or vital or anything. Small things. That I was sorry for what happened to us. That I was well and that I would look after him as best I could. (*Pause*) Mostly that I would remember her.

McKEEVER   Gone but not forgotten.

ELIZABETH   What?

McKEEVER   My father. It's what he used to write on the bill.

ELIZABETH   How is he?

McKEEVER   Singing probably — in the Heavenly Choir.

ELIZABETH   I'm sorry. I didn't know.

McKEEVER   The year after you left. Buried him in one of his own coffins. And between you and me — under the breath of course and out of deference to them that didn't know his little secret — I sang! *The Bohemian Girl*, if I remember correctly — the whole fucking lot. We all have our own way of saying goodbye, y'see.
(*Sings*) I dreamt I dwelt in marble halls
                 With vassals and serfs by my side.

Once upon a time there lived in a little town called Ballintra a man of whom it could be said was neither plain nor pretty and as happily unhappy as the day is long.

ELIZABETH I have to go, Mac. Dad will be back from the hospital soon.

McKEEVER There lived in that town also a young and very beautiful girl. When she was still a little girl, her father sent her away to the big school in the city. Why, you might ask. He was afraid, I suppose, but that's sometimes the way between the daddies and the daughters.

ELIZABETH I don't have time for playing games, Mac.

McKEEVER It's not a game, it's a fairytale. Every summer the girl would return to the sleepy town, spending her time, for she had lots of it, in the garden of the Big House where she lived or, in the evenings, walking by the seashore. The man, who had little else to do, liked to go there also. Every night, regular as clockwork, up and down the beach he'd go, counting all the white horses or waiting for the sea giants to rise up from the ocean floor and swallow him up. At first he didn't notice the girl and then, when he did, he tried not to, for she was really very young. But then . . . one evening as he passed her on the beach, the girl smiled at him and he smiled back. That was it. Nothing else, she continued on her way and he on his — but something had happened, the man had become enchanted by the beautiful princess.

ELIZABETH Get to the point, Mac.

McKEEVER I'm trying.

ELIZABETH I have to go.

McKEEVER *Please.* Not yet. I haven't finished my story.

ELIZABETH I know the end.

McKEEVER I don't.

ELIZABETH The girl was enchanted also. The rector's teenage daughter falls for the balding undertaker. No one knew, but they fell in love and lived happily ever after. Goodnight, Mac — I'll see you tomorrow.

McKEEVER Only they didn't. They fell in love all right. As deep as you can fall — but not happily ever after.

ELIZABETH You can hardly blame me for that.

McKEEVER She went away. Gone to London to see the Queen, said the Rector.

ELIZABETH You're the one who left. I took a boat to England but it was you who really disappeared.

McKEEVER Temporary retreat. Silence of the room. Not easy.

ELIZABETH I was seventeen. It wasn't easy for me either.

McKEEVER Of course not. The two of them. Needed time, that's all. Adjustments. Necessary adjustments.

ELIZABETH You said you loved me but you couldn't bring yourself to answer the 'phone.

McKEEVER Out of order. Not the 'phone. Me. Our Father who art in exile.

ELIZABETH Safe in his little room. You didn't even have the courage to tell me why.

McKEEVER Implications!

ELIZABETH What implications?

McKEEVER The young girl and the older man.

ELIZABETH Don't give me that. I knew what I was doing.

McKEEVER The man did too — that was the trouble.

ELIZABETH We were lovers, Mac — it's not a crime.

McKEEVER On the contrary — a gift from the gods!

ELIZABETH Not from the gods — from you. That's what I could never understand. Because you *did* love me, didn't you?

McKEEVER Why are you crying, the princess enquired. Because I'm happy, the man replied. Because I love you. (*Pause*) A long time ago.

ELIZABETH So bloody happy that he walked away! Oh but not without the thrilling final curtain. No conventional ending for McKeever. The climax played out on the embalming studio trolley. But you were always one for the unexpected, and it was a perfect location for the death blow, wasn't it?

McKEEVER *Contrite! The man is contrite!* (*Silence*) But it doesn't matter now.

ELIZABETH No. It doesn't. It can't. As you said — it was a long time ago. I've had to survive you. On my own. That's what your princess has become, Mac — a survivor.

ELIZABETH *exits.*

48

MCKEEVER (*Silence*) He sent her away. He didn't know why. If the bastard knew why he would have told her. And after she'd gone, the man on the trolley, cold — as fucking death.

Pause. LANGTON *has entered.*

LANGTON (*Surprised*) Mac?

MCKEEVER I came to give the sermon, John.

LANGTON At midnight?

MCKEEVER We know not the hour or the place.

LANGTON I've just seen Elizabeth. What's going on?

MCKEEVER It was a very moving sermon. Something to do with just desserts. What news of Mrs Langton?

LANGTON No change.

MCKEEVER The last lap, as they say, is the longest.

LANGTON I confess I wish it were over.

MCKEEVER Entirely understandable. It may be some consolation to know everything is in order at my end.

LANGTON Yes. I dare say. (*Pause*) Well, if there's nothing else . . .

MCKEEVER There is, actually. A favour, John. (*Pause.* LANGTON *looks at him*) Yes. Well. You'll recall our occasional conversations vis-à-vis the parallels, if you like, between religion and the theatre. Ritual elements and the like.

LANGTON Mac, it really is a bit late . . . . (*He prepares to lock up*)

MCKEEVER No. No. I don't want to talk about it. I was *thinking*, maybe we could put it to the test.

LANGTON I don't understand.

MCKEEVER A common complaint, it seems. It's all Father O'Flynn's fault, y'see. It appears he's a closet republican.

LANGTON What on earth has that got to do with me?

MCKEEVER He also has the hiring of the hall.

LANGTON Which hall?

MCKEEVER The Parish Hall.

LANGTON Get to the point, Mac.

MCKEEVER The point is, Pyramus and Thisby Productions are due to present our play in the Parish Hall on Sunday night next. Except my brave Father O'Flynn and his merry men have commandeered the kip for the musical première of the Easter Rising.

LANGTON And?

MCKEEVER And we're homeless, John. Suddenly I know what they meant by Strolling Players.

LANGTON But you know we don't have a hall.

MCKEEVER True. (*Pause*) But you do have this.

LANGTON The church? Forget it, Mac.

MCKEEVER We're desperate. I wouldn't ask if we weren't.

LANGTON It's out of the question.

He moves to exit.

MCKEEVER Think of the crowds! Be good to see a full house for Easter Sunday — you could even give a sermon.

LANGTON Don't be ridiculous. Anyway, you know well there won't be a crowd.

MCKEEVER No, I suppose not. That's not the point though. Doing it. That's the point. Same as you. Even if no one comes.

LANGTON I'm sorry, Mac.

MCKEEVER (*Desperate*) You're my last hope, John. You know what this means to me. This is *my* faith — *my* redemption.

Silence. LANGTON *stares at him. Looks around the church and back to* MCKEEVER. *Throws him the keys.*

LANGTON Lock up.

LANGTON *goes to exit door.*

MCKEEVER John? (LANGTON *turns*) God still lives in this house.

LANGTON Does he?

LANGTON *exits.* MCKEEVER *looks up.*

MCKEEVER Don't you, God? (*Pause*) Believe. Believe and you shall not be found wanting.

He blows out candle. Blackout. End of Act One.

ACT TWO

Scene One

The church. Easter Sunday morning. The rehearsal. Seating altered to create playing area for performance. A large cloth upstage as backdrop draped across church windows. Two fairly ancient theatre lights on stands, props, costumes etc. strewn about the floor. The overall impression being of a space radically transformed.

McKEEVER bursts through doors and rushes to plug in theatre lamps, singing merrily as he does, turns on tape machine at altar which plays Elizabethan ceremonial music. He rushes to exit as music continues and quickly returns wearing regal cloak and crown and accompanied by BRIDGET dressed in appropriate costume. The entrance is very big and McKEEVER in his element smiles benignly at his imaginary court. They proceed to pulpit, McKEEVER joining BRIDGET there after he turns off tape machine. What follows is an enactment of Act Five, Scene One, of A Midsummer Night's Dream.

MCKEEVER Is there no play, to ease the anguish of a torturing
            hour? Call Philostrate!

MICHAEL (*Rushes in*) Here, mighty Theseus.

MCKEEVER Say, what abridgement have you for this evening?
            What mask? What music? How shall we beguile
            The lazy time, if not with some delight?

MICHAEL There is a brief how many sports are ripe:
            Make choice of which your highness will see first.

        Silence. McKEEVER waits. Nothing. Then gestures impatiently for MICHAEL to approach him. MICHAEL goes towards organ loft and unfolds the first of a series of scrolls.

        (*Reads*) The battle with the Centaurs, to be sung

By the Athenian eunuch to the harp.

MCKEEVER We'll none of that: that have I told my love,
In glory of my kinsman Hercules.

MICHAEL The thrice three Muses mourning for the death
Of Learning, late deceas'd in beggary.

MCKEEVER That is some satire, keen and critical,
Not sorting with a nuptial ceremony!

MICHAEL A tedious brief scene of young Pyramus
And his love Thisby; very tragical mirth.

MCKEEVER Merry and tragical! Tedious and brief!
That is, hot ice and wondrous strange snow.
How shall we find the concord of this discord?
What are they that do play it?

MICHAEL Hard-handed men, that work in Athens here,
Which never labour'd in their minds till now;
And now have toil'd their unbreath'd memories
With this same play, against your nuptial.

MCKEEVER And we will hear it.

MICHAEL No, my noble lord;
It is not for you: I have heard it over,
And it is nothing, nothing in the world.

MCKEEVER I will hear that play;
For never anything can be amiss,
When simpleness and duty tender it.
Go, bring them in (*Gestures to empty space*) and take
your places, ladies.

MICHAEL *exits.*

BRIDGET (*As Hippolyta*) I love not to see wretchedness
o'ercharged,
And duty in his service perishing.

MCKEEVER Trust me. Love and tongue-tied simplicity,
In least speak most, to my capacity.

MICHAEL *returns as Philostrate.*

MICHAEL So please your grace, the Prologue is address'd.

MCKEEVER Let him approach.

MCKEEVER *goes to tape recorder and plays fanfare.*
Nothing happens.

Let him approach.

He turns off tape, sings fanfare. Nothing. MCKEEVER
furious.

Griffin!

GRIFFIN *enters somewhat self-consciously wearing*
Peter Quince's costume, bows to MCKEEVER, *turns to*
face 'Audience', stubs out cigarette end on church
floor.

GRIFFIN (*Double quick. Sing song intonation*)
If we offend, it is with our good will.
That you should think, we come not to offend,
But with good will. To show our simple skill,
That is the true beginning of our end.
Consider then, we come but in despite.
We do not come as minding to content you,
Our true intent is. All for your delight,
We are not here. That you should here repent you,
The actors are at hand; and, by their show,
You shall know all, that you are like to know.

MCKEEVER *comes down from pulpit. A long slow crawl.*

MCKEEVER Yes. Very good, Michael. Thank you, Griffin. To show
our simple skill, that is the true beginning of our end.
Now. Let's just . . . stop for a moment and examine
what we're all trying to achieve here. Bridget —
purpose of Act Five?
BRIDGET To resolve the whole plot. To denote the lapse of time.
To introduce the performance of the Rude Mechani-
cals and to give a fuller portrait of Theseus.
MCKEEVER Good. Who are the Rude Mechanicals? Michael?
MICHAEL Peter Quince, Carpenter, Nick Bottom, Weaver,
Francis Flute, Bellows Mender, Snug, Starveling and

	Snout — simple men all. Country people just like our-selves.
MCKEEVER	And what are these country people, just like our-selves, about to do? Griffin?
GRIFFIN	I wasn't here that night, boss.
MCKEEVER	Bridget?
BRIDGET	They've come to perform the merry tragedy of Pyramus and Thisby before an ungrateful court.
MCKEEVER	Good. What is the purpose of the Rude Mechanicals' play-within-a-play?

A pause. MCKEEVER *looks at them in turn.*

GRIFFIN	Relief.
MCKEEVER	I beg your pardon?
GRIFFIN	Light relief.
MCKEEVER	(*Surprised*) Very good, Griffin.
BRIDGET	(*Not to be outdone*) It is a burlesque which stands out in strong contrast to the tender and delicate play of the Fairies.
MCKEEVER	Bravo, Bridget. Now, Griffin, at this point in the proceedings *you* as Peter Quince, *as* Prologue, are introducing the dumb show which precedes the merry tragedy of Pyramus and Thisby which is about to be performed by the Rude Mechanicals who are country people just like ourselves! 'Our simple skill,' you say, 'the true beginning of our end'. But not a nursery rhyme, Griffin! Not *Jack and Jill*! Yes? And most of all, Griffin, most of all, not the fucking 3.15 at Newmarket! Let it breathe, man, let it breathe! We went through all this last week. Await the true impulse and surrender yourself to it.
GRIFFIN	Right, boss. I have ye now. Will I take another lash at it?
MCKEEVER	No. I don't think I could bear it. We'll move on to the dumb show — followed by the entrance of Pyramus and Thisby. Griffin, you'll have to play Wall. Here's the words and *this* is the costume. (*Mimes Wall using the costume*) Wall, see? The part might have been written for you. So, we'll take it from 'Gentles,

perchance you wonder at this show'.

MICHAEL (*Holding up lantern and bush*) Moonshine's gone. We've no Moonshine.

McKEEVER (*Stopped in his tracks*) Well observed, Michael. You play it.

MICHAEL But I'm playing Pyramus.

McKEEVER Pyramus and Moonshine — wonderful combination. I can see the reviews already. (MICHAEL *opens his mouth to protest*) Now don't you start.

MICHAEL I don't know his lines.

McKEEVER Then cut the fucking lines — improvise! Just carry the lantern and bush and leave the rest to me.

GRIFFIN (*With pleasure*) Lion went for a walkies as well, boss.

McKEEVER Much to your delight no doubt. I'll play Lion. Now, if nobody else has anything to gripe about, we'll proceed, shall we? Yes. Stand by for procession. I shall give you the order.

> BRIDGET *and* GRIFFIN *exit through vestry doors.* MICHAEL *is left alone with* McKEEVER *who takes off his own cloak and puts it on* MICHAEL.

(*Gently*) Stand by, Pyramus.

> *They exit through vestry door.*

Griffin, put out that cigarette. Now, you in the middle like this. And Bridget and Michael. You're on either side, like so. Wonderful. Now then, one two three . . .

> *We hear them offstage singing a slow tempo version of* Greensleeves. *At the end of the first refrain we hear* McKEEVER's *shout: 'Allegro'. The tempo increases as they enter singing and proceed in a circle around the stage before ending up in a line in front of the altar. As* GRIFFIN *speaks the Prologue, the others enact the dumb show,* MICHAEL *playing Pyramus and Moonshine,* McKEEVER *playing Lion,* GRIFFIN *as Wall and* BRIDGET *as Thisby.*
> ELIZABETH *enters at back of church, she watches the*

*rehearsal unseen, at first with amusement and, as
events unfold, with growing concern.*

GRIFFIN Gentles, perchance you wonder at this show;
But wonder on, till truth makes all things plain.
This man is Pyramus, (MICHAEL *bows*) if you would
know;
This beauteous lady, (BRIDGET *bows*) Thisby is certain.
This man, with lime and rough-cast, doth present
Wall, (MCKEEVER *pushes* GRIFFIN *forward.* GRIFFIN *bows*)
that vile Wall which did these lovers sunder;
And through Wall's chink, poor souls, they are
content
To whisper; (GRIFFIN *mimes chink in wall,* BRIDGET *and*
MICHAEL *stoop to look through chink*) at the which let no
man wonder.
This man, with lantern, dog, and bush of thorn,
Presenteth Moonshine; (MICHAEL *suddenly realises he
is playing Moonshine as well as Pyramus. Panic-stricken
he discards cloak and holds up bush and lantern as
Moonshine*) For, if you will know,
By moonshine did these lovers think no scorn.
To meet at Ninus' tomb, there, there to woo.
This grisly beast, (MCKEEVER *on all fours parades as
Lion*) which Lion hight by name,
The trusty Thisby, coming first by night,
Did scare away, or rather did affright;
(BRIDGET *makes a bold entrance as Thisby, is frightened
by McKeever's Lion, drops her mantle and flees*)
And, as she fled, her mantle she did fall,
Which Lion vile with bloody mouth did stain.
Anon comes Pyramus, sweet youth and tall,
(MICHAEL *drops lantern and bush and puts on cloak.
Furious gesture to* MCKEEVER *who assumes the character
of Moonshine. The lines are now running ahead of the
action and* MICHAEL *is desperately trying to stay in touch.
The effect should be of virtual pandemonium with the
rehearsal in complete disarray*)
And finds his trusty Thisby's mantle slain:
Whereat, with blade, with bloody blameful blade,

He bravely broach'd his boiling bloody breast;
(MICHAEL *stabs himself and collapses*)
And Thisby, tarrying in mulberry shade,
His dagger drew, and died. (BRIDGET *stabs herself and collapses*) For all the rest,
Let Lion, Moonshine, Wall, and lovers twain,
At large discourse, while here they do remain.

MCKEEVER Excellent. Some slight technical problems, I concede, but never mind, love is blind. Who's next?

BRIDGET You are, Mac.

MCKEEVER Am I?

BRIDGET Theseus. 'I wonder if the lion'.

MCKEEVER Ah yes. (*Rushes towards pulpit*) I wonder if the lion . . .

MICHAEL This is no bloody use.

MCKEEVER (*Back to* MICHAEL) Do not despair, Michael.

MICHAEL (*Throws down cloak*) No bloody use at all.

MCKEEVER (*Leads* MICHAEL *to the altar, takes cloak, rushes to pulpit*) Believe, Michael, and you shall not be found wanting.

MICHAEL (*Retreating into himself*) Ardglass, Kilmore, Farranstown, Ardbeg . . .

MCKEEVER Theseus, yes. I wonder if the lion be to speak. And Demetrius replies . . . (*Comes down from pulpit to become Demetrius*) No wonder, my Lord: one lion may when many asses do. Nice one, Demetrius — we could do with a laugh. And then, then we have Wall. (*Pause*) Wall, Griffin!

GRIFFIN Right, boss, Wall it is.

MICHAEL (*Continuing quietly but with growing intensity*) Ardglass, Kilmore, Farranstown, Ardbeg . . .

GRIFFIN (*Reading from scrap of paper* MCKEEVER *has given him — as Wall*) In this same interlude it doth befall,
That I, one Snout by name, present a wall;
And such a wall, as I would have you think,
That had in it a crannied hole or chink,
Through which the lovers, Pyramus and Thisby,
Did whisper often very secretly.
This lime, this rough-cast, and this stone, doth show
That I am that same wall; the truth is so:
And this the cranny is, right and sinister,
Through which the fearful lovers are to whisper.

MCKEEVER (*As Theseus*) Would you desire lime and hair to speak better?
(*As Demetrius*) It is the wittiest partition that ever I heard discourse, my Lord.
(*As Theseus*) Pyramus draws near the wall: silence!

> *And there is.* MCKEEVER *looks at* MICHAEL *who meets his look.* MCKEEVER *takes cloak and crosses to* MICHAEL. *He drapes* MICHAEL *with cloak.*

Pyramus draws near the wall. Silence.

MICHAEL (*After a moment he rises up as Pyramus, slowly, quietly and with true impulse, he approaches Wall*)
Oh, grim-look'd night! Oh, night with hue so black!
Oh, night, which ever art when day is not!
I fear my Thisby's promise is forgot!
And thou, oh, wall, oh, sweet, oh, lovely wall,
That stand'st between her father's ground and mine!
Show me thy chink, to blink through with mine eyne.
(*The others are aware of a depth and resonance not previously felt to his performance of these lines.* GRIFFIN *holds up his fingers to represent chink in wall*)
Thanks, courteous wall: Jove shield thee well for this!

> *The mood is suddenly and very violently interrupted when the bulb from one of the ancient lamps blows.* MICHAEL *continues but with no real impulse, his anger and despair returning.*

But what see I? No Thisby do I see.

> *The second lamp blows. This is* MICHAEL'*s final straw. He hurls these last lines at* MCKEEVER.

Oh, wicked wall, through whom I see no bliss!
Curs'd be thy stones for thus deceiving me!

> *He rips off costume. To* MCKEEVER:

Bastard! Bastard! I hate you!

MICHAEL *exits in blind fury.*

MCKEEVER (*Almost defeated now*) Yes. Such a strong word that.

> *The cloth at back wall collapses.* MCKEEVER *sees* ELIZABETH *for the first time, goes to one of the lamps.*

MCKEEVER Slight technical problem. (*Examines lamp*) Nothing too serious. Remind me to have these seen to, Griffin. (*Picks up Michael's costume*) Yes.

BRIDGET He'll come back, Mac.

GRIFFIN (*Getting out of costume*) If he had any fuckin' sense, he wouldn't. But shur poor Mikey was missin' when they were givin' out that. (*Pause*) Maybe he wasn't the only one.

> GRIFFIN *exits.*

BRIDGET They'll come back, Mac. I know they will.

MCKEEVER (*Looks again at* ELIZABETH. BRIDGET *observes this*) We'll see. Time, y'know. Not on our side now.

BRIDGET It's only eleven o'clock. We're not until eight. We've loads of time yet, Mac.

MCKEEVER We'll see.

BRIDGET (*Glances at* ELIZABETH. *Proud of this shared moment with* MCKEEVER) An act of faith. You said we must all have it.

MCKEEVER And you were not found wanting.

BRIDGET That's the past tense, Mr McKeever.

MCKEEVER Yes. Take five, Bridget. As they say.

BRIDGET Do you not want to do a few scenes?

MCKEEVER No. Not now.

BRIDGET (*Again. A quick dart to* ELIZABETH) I'll stay. Give you a hand to tidy up.

MCKEEVER *No.*

BRIDGET We'll have to hang the banner again. There's loads to do.

MCKEEVER (*Snaps at her*) Do it later! (*Softens*) I'll call you later.

BRIDGET (*Broken*) Do, so. You know where I'll be.

BRIDGET *exits. Silence.* McKEEVER *begins to tidy away costumes, props etc.*

ELIZABETH You all right?

McKEEVER Never better.

ELIZABETH I'm sorry, Mac.

McKEEVER For what?

ELIZABETH This.

McKEEVER Your fault, is it?

ELIZABETH You know what I mean.

McKEEVER It wouldn't matter. It wouldn't matter only he went so close. To soaring. (*Pause*) Poor simple Michael was almost transformed, the magic almost happened. Oh, grim look'd night! Oh, night with hue so black! (*Laughs*) No one knows the darkness more than that child. He almost found, and for the first time in his life, a voice.

ELIZABETH Is that what you want to give him?

McKEEVER It's what he's looking for — what he demands of me. A way of breaking the awful silence. A sort of . . .

ELIZABETH Healing?

McKEEVER Yes. If you like.

ELIZABETH And what are you looking for?

McKEEVER It passes the time. Nothing else. Only we seem to have run out of that commodity.

Silence. McKEEVER *examines the other lamp.*

ELIZABETH About the other night, Mac?

McKEEVER (*Sings*) Fond memories bring the light
Of other days around me . . . .

ELIZABETH Fair enough. I have to go to the hospital. If you don't want to talk —

McKEEVER About what?

ELIZABETH You know bloody well. Things got a bit heated. Maybe we both said things we shouldn't have.

McKEEVER I didn't. Did you?

ELIZABETH Look, I'm only going to be here for a few days. I would like us to be friends.

McKEEVER Friends! Oh yes. That'd be nice. Don't have many of those.

ELIZABETH Stop feeling sorry for yourself.

McKEEVER There's your father, of course. Not exactly friends. But something. The long winter evenings, hot ports in the rectory study, the shared knowledge never spoken. Our separate but secretly mutual grief for the lost princess.

ELIZABETH Do you still love me, Mac?

Silence. McKEEVER *petrified. Then quickly back to work on lamp.*

McKEEVER An act of faith she said. (*By rote*) Oh my God, I believe in you and in all you teach, because your word is true.

ELIZABETH You do, don't you?

McKEEVER He should have held a service here today — just to spite the buggers. Tried to persuade him but to no avail.

Long silence. Activity with lamp grinds slowly to a halt. He turns to her.

Yes. The nail on the head.

Silence.

ELIZABETH Then why did you let me go?

McKEEVER I told you. Temporary retreat, that's all. Would have come round. *Did* come round.

ELIZABETH When *I* was conveniently gone.

McKEEVER No. (*Silence*) Yes. I hid in the house until you left. It was appalling, unforgiveable. I'm sorry. All gone. All for the best. End of story, the lost princess.

ELIZABETH Only there was no princess, was there, Mac? And the man, our erstwhile Prince Charming was revealed in all his glory — a frightened middle-aged mortician with his trousers round his ankles on an embalming studio trolley. Not a pretty picture, is it? Not the stuff of fairytales. (*Gesturing to theatre stuff*) Not this, Mac — but the real world and all its consequences.

MCKEEVER Didn't give tuppence for consequence.
ELIZABETH Didn't you? For the public disgrace?
MCKEEVER No!
ELIZABETH For the pointing fingers, the sneering faces?
MCKEEVER Couldn't care less.
ELIZABETH For what my father would think?
MCKEEVER Didn't care.
ELIZABETH Didn't you?
MCKEEVER (*Shouts*) No! Not them! Not that!
ELIZABETH I didn't either, Mac. Because I loved you.

> *Silence.*

MCKEEVER Yes. I know. Mac and Lizzie. The happiest days. Too good to be true. (*Walks away from her*) Oh Lord I am not worthy.
ELIZABETH No more parables, Mac. Talk to me!
MCKEEVER I'm trying, Lizzie. The words. Not easy. Afraid, y'see. Of what I found. The gift. Couldn't be for me. Must be some mistake, says I. (*Pause*) Or, if thou follow me, Do not believe, but I shall do thee mischief in the wood. (*Pause*) Yes. Safe. Playing safe.

> LANGTON *enters. The silence which follows should tell us that Mrs Langton has died. No one moves. After a moment,* ELIZABETH *goes to her father, embraces him.*

ELIZABETH Of all days. The resurrection.

> ELIZABETH *looks at* MCKEEVER. *Exits.*

MCKEEVER I'm sorry, John.
LANGTON Yes. I know that.
MCKEEVER I'll do what must be done. (*About to exit*)
LANGTON A blessed release.

> MCKEEVER *stops.*

Isn't that what they say? What *I*'d say at times like this. What other platitudes spring to mind, McKeever? God has called her home — that always went down well. Or, she died a happy death — as if there was such a thing. But who cares when it's third party grief. Nothing like your own to expose the hollow core of priestly sympathy.

MCKEEVER   You were never a hypocrite, John.

LANGTON   Wasn't I? Elizabeth is right. Of all days, to die on the morning of the resurrection. Was it Margaret's parting gift, I wonder? A final seed of doubt. Year after year I stood in that pulpit on Easter morning and preached the ultimate message of hope. Christ has died, Christ is risen, Christ will come again. Only in truth I didn't believe it — and haven't done for many years. And I think finally they knew, that small impoverished community gathered before me in His name; they knew I didn't believe in it anymore than they did. But we endured. Year after year in a conspiracy of silence, kindling the flames of a half-remembered faith, gathered more for consolation than in hope — Our kingdom of this, and not the next world. (*Pause*) When you close the lid on Margaret's coffin, Mac, I do not expect to see her again. If I believe that, then it's no bad thing this church is closing. I won't preach again.

MCKEEVER   Preach. One more time. (*Pause.* LANGTON *looks at him*) Margaret's funeral. Her parting gift.

LANGTON   No. The church in Kiltown will receive her this evening. She'll be buried there tomorrow.

MCKEEVER   Here. In this place. You'll bury her here, John.

LANGTON   I said no. You have my instructions, McKeever — I expect you to carry them out.

MCKEEVER   Mac knows best. Always did.

LANGTON   Not this time. This isn't one of your damned plays, McKeever.

MCKEEVER   Yes. Well, we'll see. Now, I must get to the hospital.

LANGTON   You don't understand.

MCKEEVER   Why do we have to understand, John? Faith — any manner of — blind. We can't all poke our grubby fingers in his side. There wouldn't be room. So. You believe, even when you don't see. Whistle in the dark and hope — *hope!* — for the best. I'll ring you later after I've taken care of Margaret.

LANGTON Why are you doing this?

McKEEVER I don't know. For you maybe. The last act. A requiem.

> *Silence.* McKEEVER *exits.* LANGTON *alone. A beat. Then crosses to pulpit, ascends steps, stands facing out into empty church, takes a breath, as though about to speak, but nothing comes out, turns and descends steps as lights fade to blackout.*

ACT TWO

Scene Two

A little later. McKeever's embalming studio. As lights fade on church a lighting grid is lowered on playing area for studio. Background music at very low level. As grid is lowered, McKEEVER enters brisk and businesslike, wheeling in the remains of Mrs Langton. Her body draped in a white sheet and lying on a trolley. He places the trolley directly under the harsh white light of the grid.

McKEEVER *(Singing happily on entrance)*
E'er since by faith I saw the stream,
Thy flowing wounds supply
Redeeming love has been my theme
And shall be till I die.

> *He pulls sheet back from her face. During the following sequence he washes and dries the face and hands, packs the orifices of ears and nose and applies massage cream to face and hands.*

Enfin, le visage! Hands and face, the most important. Visible signs, d'y'see. So. No cock-ups in that department. And there won't be either — not tonight, Josephine! *(Water and cloth at base of trolley)* The embalmer, Margaret, is a creator of illusions. We banish the traces of suffering and death and present the deceased in an attitude of normal and restful sleep. We create, as Strub and Frederick so movingly put it, 'a memory picture'. Good old Strub and Frederick, the unsung heroes of the mortuary. Perhaps you've heard of them, Margaret. Their book, *The Principles and Practice of Embalming* is the veritable bible of our profession. Not exactly coffee table stuff, I grant you, and I don't expect they'll surface in the bestseller lists, but old Strub and Frederick have filled many a lonely hour for me, I can tell you. (*Pause*) There now, clean as a new pin. (*Forceps and cotton wool*) Next, we have the packing of the orifices. Don't worry, Margaret, you won't feel a thing. (*Pause*) You don't mind if I call you Margaret, do you, Margaret? I feel it brings us closer. And after all, I was almost one of the family one time, wasn't I? Of course, you couldn't have known that and I don't suppose it matters to you now but I was, yes, very much so.

Pause. Takes remote control switch from pocket and turns off music.

We were lovers, y'see. Lizzie and me. That shocked you, didn't it — if you were alive today you'd die of the fright. Yes, lovers. In this very room too. On this very trolley. Life and death. Would have told you sooner only I didn't think you'd understand. That's why she went away. Nothing to do with you or John, Margaret — it was all McKeever's fault. (*Pause*) Don't be angry, Margaret — I meant no harm. Please. Don't get upset. It was all right. (*Pause*) It was all right, that is, until I blew it. I couldn't cut it, Margaret. And the track record, not great. Ask the absent Mrs McKeever if you don't believe me. Didn't want to repeat history, did we? So I rewrote it instead. Our father who art in exile, that was me. Never around when he's wanted. (*Sings*) I see the moon, the moon sees me
Under the shade of the old oak tree.
Please let the moon that shines on me
Shine on the one I love.

MICHAEL *enters.*

Ah, Michael. Just in time. Massage cream. Purpose A?

MICHAEL (*Without enthusiasm*) To keep the skin soft and natural.

MCKEEVER B?

MICHAEL   To stimulate circulation.

McKEEVER   Excellent! And C?

MICHAEL   I don't remember.

McKEEVER   Of course you do.

MICHAEL   I don't remember, I said.

McKEEVER   C. To retard dehydration. Dehydration, Michael, the great enemy of the embalmer. And D?

MICHAEL   Me father said to say I'm sorry.

McKEEVER   D. To create a suitable cosmetic base. I never use make-up, of course.

MICHAEL   He said I had no right to run away.

McKEEVER   Male or female. That's where the lights come in, you see. A nice rose-tinted gel is your only man.

MICHAEL   You're not listening to me.

McKEEVER   Hanging on every word, Michael. Tell your father there's no need to apologise; you had good reason to run. Now, closing the mouth. Purpose?

MICHAEL   (*Sullen*) To create feature naturalness and for cosmetic effect.

McKEEVER   Expand. The mouth is a highly important feature . . .

MICHAEL   From the standpoint of appearance as it is the most expressive feature of a dead face. If the mouth is improperly positioned, the entire facial expression and appearance will be unsatisfactory.

McKEEVER   Excellent. My first and final apprentice. When I shuffle off this mortal coil, Michael, I shall expect *you* to embalm *me*.

MICHAEL   I can't do it, Mr McKeever.

McKEEVER   Of course you can. You're learning more every day.

MICHAEL   The play, I mean.

McKEEVER   Nonsense. You're just nervous, that's all. We all are. All four of us.

MICHAEL   Three. Griffin's above in the Protestant graveyard.

McKEEVER   Yes, but he's not burying *himself*, is he? I sent him up to dig Mrs Langton's grave.

MICHAEL   He says he'll not be here tonight.

Pause.

McKEEVER   He won't need to be. I've let you down, Michael. The magic spell didn't work — we will, none of us, be transformed. There'll be a funeral, not a play, in the church tonight. (*Silence*) You were very good this morning, Michael.

MICHAEL *glares at him.*

Would I lie to you?

MICHAEL You did about the sea giants. There's no such thing.

MCKEEVER Isn't there?

MICHAEL Griffin laughed at me when I told him about them. And anyway, I looked for days and never seen them.

MCKEEVER That's because they only come out at night. Just because you don't see them doesn't mean they're not there, you know.

MICHAEL I don't believe you.

Silence. MCKEEVER *sees that he means it.*

MCKEEVER Then don't.

MICHAEL You're only coddin' me. Same as everyone do.

MCKEEVER Does.

MICHAEL Does. I used to think you were different. The crowd that laughs at Mikey is one thing. But I thought you were another. My father said you were a good man. That's why he asked ye to put me playactin' and helpin' y'out in the shop with the coffins. He said that you were a good man, that'd look after me and show me things. But my father was wrong. You're not. You'd have me be the fool the same as the rest of them, laughing and skittering when I pass in the street, callin' me names behind me back. 'Mad Mikey'! 'Mad Mikey' they call me. And you're no different. Only you'd have me be the fool on a stage, where everyone could see me. He said to tell you I was sorry and I am. But I won't do it.

Silence.

MCKEEVER I'm sorry too. To have failed you. Go home, Michael.

Tell your father the apology is mine.

Silence. They look at one another. MICHAEL *exits.* MCKEEVER *looks at the corpse and covers the head with the sheet.*

The embalmer, Margaret, is the creator and destroyer of illusions.

He is gone.

ACT TWO

Scene Three

As MCKEEVER *exits, lights fade on embalming studio and up on church.*
ELIZABETH'S *organ music is heard as* MCKEEVER'S *voice fades away.*
   This continues for a few moments. LANGTON *enters upstage and comes slowly down.* ELIZABETH *finishes hymn.*

LANGTON I'm sorry — I didn't mean to interrupt.

ELIZABETH You didn't. A little self-indulgent sentiment, that's all. It was her favourite hymn.

LANGTON You play beautifully. Just as she did.

ELIZABETH No. Not like her at all. (*Pause*) Are you all right?

LANGTON Yes. It's just the waiting. And you?

ELIZABETH Okay.

LANGTON McKeever rang just now.

ELIZABETH What did he want?

LANGTON He'd like us to go to the funeral parlour — before they close the coffin.

ELIZABETH How many times do we have to say goodbye?

LANGTON You don't have to. I'll call him back.

ELIZABETH No. We'll go.

LANGTON He wants to hold the burial service here.

ELIZABETH It isn't his decision.

LANGTON That man Griffin has already dug a grave.

ELIZABETH They'll dig another in Kiltown. It's your decision.

LANGTON What do *you* think?

ELIZABETH What I think doesn't matter. You're the only one who can decide.

LANGTON The Church won't recognise the service.

ELIZABETH So, what will they do? Dig her up again when your back is turned.

LANGTON Please, Elizabeth.

ELIZABETH You want to bury her here, don't you? Then do it.

LANGTON God knows it's all the same to your mother. Put me down in a tea chest, she said once. Somewhere between the orchard and the rhododendrons. I think she meant it too.

ELIZABETH You'll miss her very much, won't you?

LANGTON Yes. Though I've had plenty of practice. After you left your mother closed a door on the world. I managed to break in from time to time, but she didn't encourage visitors.

ELIZABETH Do you think she forgave me?

LANGTON There was nothing to forgive, Elizabeth.

ELIZABETH I wanted to ask her. But I was too late.

LANGTON She never judged you. Neither of us had the right to do that.

ELIZABETH If I'd stayed she might still be alive today.

LANGTON You can't take responsibility for that.

ELIZABETH It's what I feel. And this. I might have helped keep it open.

LANGTON What's ordained is ordained. All that matters is that we try to find peace. It's a very elusive state, isn't it?

ELIZABETH Yes. (*Pause*) We'd better tidy up. Mac's hardly going to need all this now, is he?

They begin to gather up props, costumes etc.

LANGTON We've hardly spoken since you came home, Elizabeth.

ELIZABETH There hasn't been time.

LANGTON Is that the only reason? I get the feeling you've been avoiding me. And when we do meet we behave like perfect strangers.

ELIZABETH Isn't that what we are now?

LANGTON Yes, I suppose so. You're still my daughter — all I have left now.

ELIZABETH I know. I'll stay as long as you need me.

LANGTON Or as long as *you* need *me*. There's a great trouble in your heart, Elizabeth.

ELIZABETH I'd better go.

LANGTON Tell *him* what's in your heart. (*Elizabeth stunned*) Don't look so surprised. What's left of a paternal instinct maybe.

ELIZABETH I'm sorry, Dad.

LANGTON For what? Daring to love? McKeever's a good man, Elizabeth. Somewhat wayward without doubt, but a good man. My only regret is that your mother and I were not the sort of people you could have spoken to about this. It might have saved some pain.

ELIZABETH Did he tell you?

LANGTON Not in so many words. We had a sort of unspoken agreement never to air the subject. (*Smiles*) Your ghost would sit between us like an unexploded bomb — liable to detonate and destroy us at the very mention of your name! I regret now that I allowed him to suffer in silence for so long. I was afraid I'd lose him too, I suppose.

He goes to her. They embrace.

There now. Everything will be fine. I promise you. (*Pause*) I'll always be here for you, Elizabeth. And so, I shouldn't wonder, will McKeever.

ELIZABETH It's not that simple.

LANGTON No. I suppose not. I don't know what's going on between you two, but I do know you must speak your heart. Speak your heart, Elizabeth. I know from bitter experience that the price of silence is very high.

ELIZABETH Are you coming?

LANGTON No. You go.

ELIZABETH Don't you want to see her?

LANGTON No. It's too late for that. You go.

Pause. ELIZABETH *exits.*

Misfits. (*Pause*) Misfits all.

Lights fade.

ACT TWO

Scene Four

McKeever's funeral parlour. As lights come up MCKEEVER *enters wheeling in the open coffin of Mrs Langton. He is followed by* GRIFFIN *wheeling in a small table, bearing McKeever's jacket, bowler hat and a bunch of fresh bluebells.*

MCKEEVER (*Standing back to admire his handiwork*) Consummatum est! What do you think, Griffin?

GRIFFIN You took the words out of me mouth, boss — Consummatum is right. Shur she's like a new woman. Begod, if you asked that wan nicely, she might sit up and take tea.

MCKEEVER Indeed. Mrs Langton's tea-drinking days are over, Griffin.

GRIFFIN Not that 'twas tea has her where she's lying now. If you receive me meaning.

MCKEEVER No, Griffin, I don't.

> *He makes adjustments to head of corpse, arranges frills etc., adjusts hands.*

GRIFFIN They say she was pickled. In whisky like. I'm not one to talk, mind, but the word was she took bad after the youngwan left.

> *He watches* MCKEEVER *for the effect of this.* MCKEEVER *ignores it, begins to set up chairs beside the coffin.*

Will two be enough?

MCKEEVER Two what?

GRIFFIN Chairs. I don't suppose there'll be many up. The

73

Proddies don't go in much for showin' off the corpse. (MCKEEVER *does not respond*) Two it is, so. (GRIFFIN *lights up cigarette and sits in one of the chairs*) I see she's home.

MCKEEVER 'She', Griffin? To whom are you referring?

GRIFFIN The Langton youngwan. That was her above in the church.

MCKEEVER Is that so?

GRIFFIN And well you know it. Shur weren't you and her pally one time, boss? About the time your missus ran off with the dancer, wasn't it? A bit of company I suppose — though she was awful young.

MCKEEVER Thank you, Griffin. That will be all.

GRIFFIN D'y'know what, boss? Her nibs there and Lizzie. That was her name, wasn't it? They're the spittin' image of one another. The minute I copped her above in the church, I said to myself that wan's a ringer for poor Mrs Langton. The bird, says I, is back to the nest.

MCKEEVER I said that will be all, Griffin.

GRIFFIN And I was going to ask her, for the crack like, about the time she went away. Did she walk — or was she pushed?

MCKEEVER *Get out!*

GRIFFIN Something wrong, boss?

MCKEEVER *Leave!* Before I throw you out.

GRIFFIN Jaysus, you're awful prickly. Shur amn't I only slaggin' ye. Doesn't the whole fuckin' town know ye gave her a babby.

MCKEEVER Scum. Fucking scum! How dare you. *How dare you!*

GRIFFIN Aisy, boss. Not in front of the corpse. You're not in one of your fucking plays now, you know. And I wouldn't go throwing names around either. For all your high-falutin' notions, you're the same scum as the rest of us. A fuckin' nobody like meself.

MCKEEVER Please. Go. *Now.*

GRIFFIN I'll go when I'm good and ready, McKeever.

MCKEEVER This parlour. A place of sanctity. Respect, Griffin. Respect for the dead.

GRIFFIN Fuck the dead. Fuck the livin' an' the dead. That's what I say. Parlour my arse. Bloody sideshow morelike,

with your lights and your music and the fuck knows
what else. This shite won't save you, McKeever, no
more than your plays will.

MCKEEVER Yes.

*He sings 'I See the Moon'. Back to corpse. Frenetic
attempt to settle himself. Adjusting position of corpse,
standing back to view it, back to corpse etc. This
continues during* GRIFFIN's *speech, consciously trying
to block what* GRIFFIN *is saying, until he can no longer
do so and turns to face him.*

GRIFFIN I coulda told ye, y'know. The way I told Mad Mikey
and frigid Bridget. Coulda told ye your two-bit
fuckin' farcehole play would never see the light of
day. They were aisy fooled, weren't they, with all your
grand talk of transformation. The spirit will come
upon you and you will be changed into a different
person. Like fuck we would. You didn't change me,
McKeever, but you didn't fool me either. I was too
cute for you and when the boys downtown'd take the
piss the greenbacks you gave me would always shut
them up. You didn't change me. My sort, never
anything but nobodies. But I'm cute, McKeever. I can
see where bread is buttered and you buttered mine
nicely for a while. But you didn't fool me, d'y'hear?
Not for a fuckin' second. And you won't change me,
no more than you'll change yourself. (*Pause*) The
difference between us, *boss* — the difference is, I
know. I know what I am.

GRIFFIN *goes to leave.*

MCKEEVER And what about the German boy, Griffin? Did you
know what you were, that night last summer, with the
German boy against the wall in Seafield?

GRIFFIN No!

MCKEEVER Oh, yes. I don't miss much either. My perambulations. Did you know then what you were?

GRIFFIN No. Not me. Not me.

MCKEEVER Oh, it was you all right. Never more *truly*, I should think. I was surprised, Griffin, not shocked, but surprised. Because I didn't think you'd have the courage. And to love in that way in this place *is* a rare form of courage.

GRIFFIN Not love. Hate. Hate. I fuckin' hate!

MCKEEVER No, not hate, Griffin. He held you in his arms and you cried. Not hate. No more lies, Griffin.

GRIFFIN If you ever . . . if you ever tell anyone what you saw I'll kill you. D'y'hear?

MCKEEVER Our little secret, Griffin. Safe with me. But it was why I asked you to do the play — even if I did have to pay for the privilege. Not to change you, but in some small way to let you try to be yourself.

GRIFFIN I was drunk.

MCKEEVER Yes.

GRIFFIN Bastard led me on.

MCKEEVER Yes.

GRIFFIN Aisy for him. Just passin' through. All the one to him, the bastard. Whatever came over me. Never happened before. Or since. I swear. Just the once, McKeever. (*Pause*) Only lonely, y'know. No company. Not that shower o' cunts down the town. Not that sort. Real company. (*Crying*) Love, y'know. Just the once. Love.

MCKEEVER (*Goes to him*) Yes. Love.

GRIFFIN If you ever . . .

MCKEEVER I know, Griffin, I know.

> GRIFFIN *exits.* MCKEEVER *watches him go before retreating to what we assume is a room off parlour.* BRIDGET *enters, looks around, goes to the head of the coffin. As she is about to touch the face of the corpse* MCKEEVER *returns carrying a pair of rose-tinted lighting gels.*

BRIDGET She's looking well.

MCKEEVER Bit of a rush job, Bridget. But I must say I am rather pleased.

BRIDGET So is her daughter. Looking well, I mean.

MCKEEVER That so? I didn't really notice.

BRIDGET Didn't you?

MCKEEVER No.

> *He gestures to her to sit. She does so. He lowers lighting grid with remote control console and begins to fit the gels.*

BRIDGET What's wrong with Griffin?

MCKEEVER Nothing much. A little lovesick maybe. He's never been better.

BRIDGET (*Laughs*) Griffin lovesick? Shur who'd have him.

MCKEEVER You'd never know, Bridget.

BRIDGET I suppose she's home for the funeral.

MCKEEVER Who?

BRIDGET Elizabeth.

MCKEEVER Yes. In fact I'm expecting her over at any moment. With her father. To view the deceased. A very private moment.

> *Pause.*

BRIDGET You know what I'm here for. We're running out of time, Mac.

MCKEEVER I'm afraid we've already done so. There isn't going to *be* any play. (*Silence*) I'm sorry, Bridget.

BRIDGET You don't have to be. It doesn't matter.

MCKEEVER The funeral, see. Mrs Langton's remains.

BRIDGET I just wanted to know, that's all.

MCKEEVER I am sorry, Bridget.

BRIDGET You don't have to keep saying that! I know you are. And anyway, I should have known — the way the rest of them did.

MCKEEVER You kept the faith, Bridget.

BRIDGET Yes. But it was silly to. Maybe it's just as well. Michael was right. The laughing stock of Ballintra!

MCKEEVER (*Smiling*) I suppose so.

> BRIDGET *is almost in tears. He goes to her, brushes his hand tenderly against her cheek.*

I failed you, didn't I?

BRIDGET You didn't mean to. Just the way it goes, that's all. I was so looking forward to it. To *being* somebody. Somebody else. I wanted to make you proud of me.

McKEEVER You know I am.

BRIDGET No. I don't know. I wanted you to admire me. Not just you — all of them, the whole town. But especially you. And now you won't.

McKEEVER Lost. Lost in admiration!

BRIDGET No. I'm just a silly schoolgirl with a crush on teacher!

McKEEVER *kisses her, lightly and walks away from her.*

That's the consolation prize, isn't it — a kiss?

McKEEVER You're a very fine young woman, Bridget.

BRIDGET Schoolgirl. Just a silly schoolgirl.

McKEEVER Leave this place. Take flight, Bridget, soar! Before they catch you. They'll clip your wings if they do. Cut you down to size. And then where will you be? Grounded, that's where.

BRIDGET I don't want to go away — I want to stay here with you.

McKEEVER Nobody stays with me, Bridget. Impossible, y'see. Quite impossible. Our midsummer night's dream, a small vessel of hope. But scuttled, sunk without trace, as if it never existed.

BRIDGET I won't forget it.

McKEEVER Get out of this place, Bridget. There are other countries to dream in.

BRIDGET Bríd Flynn has two tickets for the pageant. I might go with her.

McKEEVER You might. But I don't think so.

BRIDGET I love you, Mr McKeever.

McKEEVER (*Touched*) Thank you. Such a big word.

BRIDGET It's only a few letters. I love you and you love her, don't you?

Silence.

McKEEVER Yes. Yes, I think I do.

BRIDGET I'll go then. (*Pause*) Thanks, Mac.

McKEEVER What for?

BRIDGET I dunno. For moonshine, maybe.

> *She exits. He watches her go, looks at coffin. Then he*
> *goes to it.*

McKEEVER Moonshine. (*Pause*) Thanks for moonshine. (*Pause*)
Imagine that, Margaret! Thanks, she said. What for,
says I — surprised. For moonshine, says she. Imagine
that. (*Pause*) I know what she meant though. And it's
something. D'y'know what, Margaret? — I feel like
singing! Don't ask me why — we don't know from
why!

> *He pushes button on console. We hear Bing Crosby's*
> *'Love is the Sweetest Thing'. As* McKEEVER *joins in the*
> *song, he continues to work with the corpse, until he is*
> *no longer able to restrain himself and begins to move in*
> *tempo with the music and finally to dance with the*
> *coffin.* ELIZABETH *enters,* McKEEVER *in full flight. He*
> *winds down when he becomes aware of her presence.*
> *He cuts music.*

Mea culpa, Elizabeth. (*Pause*) Congenital emotional
disorder, see. A compulsion to dance in the face of
death. Not exactly a virtue in my line of work, but
there you go.

ELIZABETH My father isn't coming.

McKEEVER Just you and me then.

ELIZABETH He didn't want to see her again.

McKEEVER (*Disappointed*) Unwise if I may say so. The memory
picture, you see — very important. Anyway you'll
want to be alone.

ELIZABETH No. No, stay with me.

> *She extends her hand. He looks at it as though it were*
> *some strange and perhaps frightening creature, then*
> *goes and takes her hand.*

McKEEVER Yes. I remember this; holding hands. In the dark

maybe — or was it sunlight? Doesn't matter. Nice. Very nice.

He leads her to coffin.

ELIZABETH What am I supposed to say?
McKEEVER A prayer maybe. Or goodbye. Sometimes they touch the deceased.
ELIZABETH No.
McKEEVER A little gesture. Like this.
ELIZABETH (*Recoils*) No. Close it, please.
McKEEVER You didn't look.
ELIZABETH I did.
McKEEVER The memory picture — all you have left.
ELIZABETH There is *nothing* left. Please, Mac.
McKEEVER Can't say I didn't try.

McKEEVER gets coffin lid. He is about to put the lid on coffin but waits until ELIZABETH turns away.

ELIZABETH He's going to hold the service in the church.
McKEEVER The last act. A sort of final curtain.
ELIZABETH He hasn't said so, but I know it's what he wants.
McKEEVER We should have music.
ELIZABETH No.
McKEEVER You could play the organ. Your mother's favourites.
ELIZABETH I said no.
McKEEVER Then I will. McKeever's Funeral Emporium — for the *complete* funeral service.
ELIZABETH You can't stage manage this, Mac.

Pause.

McKEEVER No. I suppose not.

Silence.

ELIZABETH She's at peace now, isn't she?
McKEEVER (*Screwing down lid. Looks at her*) I'm sure she is.
ELIZABETH Only she always wanted him to go first. The thought

	of him being left on his own used really upset her. (*Pause*) You'll look after him, won't you?
McKEEVER	The blind leading the blind.
ELIZABETH	He needs somebody.
McKEEVER	We can lean on each other's crutches. (*Pause*) When do you go back?
ELIZABETH	I don't know. In a few days maybe.
McKEEVER	Someone waiting, I suppose.
ELIZABETH	No. There's no one waiting.
McKEEVER	I do. Wait. For something to happen. For something to make sense again. Daddio on the open road, singing at the top of his voice. Wait. You have to wait.

Silence.

ELIZABETH	My father said we should always speak our hearts. It's good advice, isn't it?
McKEEVER	The best.
ELIZABETH	If not easily applied. But I will. Try to. I never stopped loving you either, Mac. (*Pause*) I want you to know that. To remember it always. I remember what you gave me. Hope. That was it. Now I want to give it back to you. So that when I'm gone you'll always have it — a candle to curse the darkness.

Silence.

McKEEVER	You could stay.
ELIZABETH	It's too late for that now.
McKEEVER	Is it? (*Pause*) Is it, Lizzie? You could stay. (*Pause*) We could make a baby. Not today, not tomorrow, but *maybe*. (*Pause*) It'd be a girl, of course. And it would have your eyes, blue eyes like the sea. We could call it Margaret — Peggy for short. (*Taps coffin*) Our very own little resurrection.

They look at each other. Silence. Lights fade.

ACT TWO

Scene Five

As lights come up on church, LANGTON *enters, dressed in appropriate funeral vestments. He takes his place before the altar.* ELIZABETH *goes to front pew and kneels.* MCKEEVER *wheels coffin before altar and takes his place to one side of pulpit.*

LANGTON (*The words spoken without conviction*)
> I am the Resurrection and the Life, saith the Lord;
> He that believeth in me, though he were dead,
> Yet shall he live: And whosoever liveth and
> Believeth in me shall never die.

> *Silence. He looks at the coffin, at* ELIZABETH, *then at the empty church and finally to* MCKEEVER.

> Yea though I walk through the valley of the shadow of
> Death, I will fear no evil:
> For thou art with me:
> Thy rod and staff comfort me.

> BRIDGET *enters.*

> But thy loving kindness and mercy shall follow me
> All the days of my life:
> And I will dwell in the house of the Lord forever.

MCKEEVER Amen.

> MICHAEL *enters and sits.* LANGTON *looks again at* MCKEEVER, *then walks to pulpit. Our understanding must be that it is becoming progressively more difficult*

for LANGTON *to carry on.*

LANGTON   As we gather this Easter Day to receive our dear sister Margaret, we recall the words of Paul in his letter to the Corinthians: O Death where is thy sting, O Grave where is thy victory. Death is swallowed up in victory.

> GRIFFIN *enters, stands at back of church.*

For those of us who mourn her, however, there is, there can be, this evening, no sense of victory. There is in our hearts a sense only of loss. We are defeated, not victorious in the face of her and of our own mortality. (*Pause*) Unless. Unless as believers, unless in faith we turn to the mystery of the Resurrection. Be not afraid, he said. Ye seek Jesus of Nazareth. He is . . . *risen.*

> *Silence.*

And so.

> *He struggles to continue, looks at the coffin, then at* MCKEEVER.

And so. (*Pause*) And so — *nothing.*

MCKEEVER   And so this evening . . . Say it, John. Say it.
LANGTON   No!
MCKEEVER   Say it. You have to. Believe in something. All of us, John. Say it.
LANGTON   (*Shouts*) *No!*

> *He descends pulpit.* ELIZABETH *rushes to his assistance.*

Nothing to say.

> *Silence.*

MCKEEVER Then I will. I'll say it. I'll believe.

He enters pulpit. Silence. He looks at LANGTON *and*
ELIZABETH, *then to* GRIFFIN, BRIDGET *and* MICHAEL.

And so this evening. Shrouded as we are in grief.
Valley of tears, dust to dust and all the rest of it. We
look at our sister Margaret and we remember the
mystery. *Et valde mane!* And early in the morning
Mary Magdalene, Mary the mother of James and
Salomé in the goodness of their hearts coming to
anoint the dead Christ. Only no sign, nowhere to be
seen. Gentle Jesus, meek and mild is missing. The
tomb is empty! The three ladies, you might say, under-
standably mortified. Bodysnatchers maybe, only
there was a guard at the door of the tomb all night.
And anyway, the same evening, He shows up for
dinner at Simon's house. Quod erat demonstrandum
— He had risen as He promised.

Pause.

We haven't seen the like of it since, John. Maybe it
was a once-off, just another party piece from a man
who knew a trick or two. (*Pause*) But maybe not.
Maybe not! And so we wait. In hope, for something to
happen. For something to make sense. Not just the
big one, the trumpet of angels, the joyful resurrection.
But in the meantime, here in this dark corner, we wait.
For a small flicker of light.

Silence. MCKEEVER *descends pulpit. After a moment or
two* MICHAEL *rises slowly, then speaks quietly and
utterly without the artifice of performance.*

MICHAEL Well, it shall be so. But there is two hard things — that
is, to bring the moonlight into a chamber; for, you
know, Pyramus and Thisby meet by moonlight.
BRIDGET (*Pause. Uncertain*) Doth the moon shine that night we
play our play?

MICHAEL Yes, it doth shine that night.

BRIDGET Why, then, may you leave a casement of the great chamber-window, where we play, open, and the moon may shine in at the casement.

MICHAEL Aye; or else one must come in with a bush of thorns and a lantern, and say he comes to disfigure, or to present, the person of moonshine. Then, there is another thing: we must have a wall in the great chamber; for Pyramus and Thisby, says the story, did talk through the chink of a wall.

BRIDGET You can never bring in a wall. (*She looks at* GRIFFIN) What say you, Bottom?

Silence.

GRIFFIN Some man or other must present wall: and let him have some plaster, or some loam, or some rough-cast about him, to signify wall; and let him hold his fingers thus, and through that cranny shall Pyramus and Thisby whisper.

MICHAEL If that may be, then all is well. Come, sit down, every mother's son, and rehearse your parts. (*To* MCKEEVER) Pyramus, you begin. When you have spoken your speech, enter into that brake — and so everyone according to his cue.

> *During the foregoing, from* MICHAEL's *lines, beginning 'Well, it shall be so,' we gradually bring down general stage lighting and bring up the two theatre lamps, so that we are left with just these and the moonlight which comes in through the windows of the church. During all this,* MCKEEVER, ELIZABETH *and* LANGTON *watch and listen in silence,* MCKEEVER *permitting himself the slightest smile as the lights fade to blackout.*